12 STEPS TO
LIVING
WITHOUT
FEAR

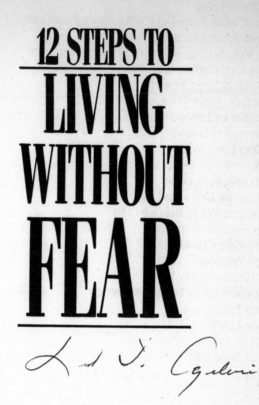

LLOYD OGILVIE

12 STEPS TO
LIVING
WITHOUT
FEAR

Let God Love you

All Scripture quotations, unless otherwise noted, are from The Holy
Bible, New King James Version, copyright © 1979, 1980, 1982 by Thomas
Nelson, Inc. Used by permission. Scripture quotations marked TLB are
from *The Living Bible*, copyright © 1971 by Tyndale House Publishers,
Wheaton, Illinois.

Library of Congress Cataloging in Publication Data

Ogilvie, Lloyd John.
    Twelve steps to living without fear.

    1. Fear—Religious aspects—Christianity.
2. Fear.   3. Christian life—Presbyterian authors.
I. Title.   II. Title: 12 steps to living without
fear.
BV4908.5.O35   1987   248.8′6   87–25305
ISBN 0–8499–0613–X

Printed in the United States of America

7898 BK 987654321

Contents

1. Fearless and Free   11
2. Children of a Looser God   29
3. A Gnawing Uneasiness   43
4. Left Luggage   59
5. Embrace Yourself   75
6. The Gift of Inadequacy   91
7. The Quicksands of Rejection   109
8. The Fear of Losing Control   129
9. It's All in Your Imagination   147
10. Fast-Forward to the Beginning   169
11. Motivating with Love   187
12. A Future without Panic   209

Notes   224

Acknowledgments

This book is a call for a new breed of counter-culture Christians to join in a conquest of fear. That battle begins within ourselves. We must conquer the deepest fears in our souls before we can help others.

Each of the chapters in this book is a step in a personal and practical twelve-step program to living without fear. We will deal with the fears that keep us from living with freedom and joy. The steps are carefully arranged to give us a progressive experience of God's fear-dispelling power. The hope is that the readers will use these steps for daily victory over fear for years to come.

I am thankful for the people who have shared the vision for this book.

Charles "Kip" Jordon, Executive Vice President, and Ernest Owen, Senior Vice President and Publisher, of Word Books were both enthusiastic cheerleaders for the concept and development of the book.

It has been a joy to work with Pat Wienandt, Senior Academic Editor, in the final preparation of my books for publication. Her editing skills, her knowledge of the biblical languages, and her keen interest in communicating Christ's power for our deepest needs always maximize any book I write.

My books are written in the flow of a busy life as Pastor of a church, media communicator, and speaker. I could not manage that challenge without the efficiency and enthusiasm of my Executive Secretary, Lynda Calhoun.

Lynne Martins, my Special Projects Secretary, who in addition to all her other responsibilities manages my publication activities, faithfully typed the manuscript through many revisions and invested her own editing skills in the project.

Any author needs many pairs of eyes to review his work so that his writing expresses clearly what is in his mind and heart. I'm privileged to have friends who help me do that: Dr. Dale Salwak, Professor of English at Citrus College in Glendora, California, friend and member of my church who provides me with reading materials to stimulate my mind and seed my soul, assisted with the editing; Georgiana Walker, seasoned editor, is an invaluable part of my team.

Special gratitude goes to William McCalmont, our church librarian, who for fifteen years has provided me with stacks of books to read each week in preparation for my preaching and writing.

When I thank all of these friends personally they respond, "It's a pleasure," and because of them the writing of this book has become a pleasure for me. I am deeply gratified for the effort of all of them in helping make this book a reality.

Lloyd Ogilvie

12 STEPS TO

LIVING

WITHOUT

FEAR

Step 1 _____

My fear is really loneliness for God.
Therefore, I will claim His promise
to never leave or forsake me.

_____

Fearless and Free

OLIVER STONE SAT BOLT UPRIGHT IN BED IN A COLD SWEAT.

Fear drenched his sheets.

A frightening dream had awakened him. A disturbing, recurring dream.

"They had shipped me back to Vietnam," he said. "Somehow they found me at 38 and sent me back. I woke up in a sweat, in total terror."[1]

Sixteen years ago movie writer and director Oliver Stone served in Vietnam, where he earned a bronze star and endured both physical and emotional wounds. Since then he's lived with the nightmare of what it was like back in an unpopular war he wishes he could forget and yet is concerned that America might too easily forget.

And so, Oliver Stone made a movie called *Platoon* about his Vietnam experience. It was a box office bonanza that gave him a cathartic release of old fears and high marks as a writer and director.

Alfred Hitchcock used to say, "The only way I get rid of my fears is to make movies of them."

You and I don't have that advantage. But we do have fears, plenty of them, and not all of them are nightmares. Some of the most troublesome are the wide-awake fears that cling to us even in broad daylight. They make us retreat from life instead of living it to the fullest.

Probing the Raw Nerve

Recently, I was interviewed in a television talk show in the Midwest by a woman who seemed to be a polished combination of Barbara Walters and Jane Pauley. She projected a "Miss Put-Together" image of personal and professional competence.

After introducing me, the woman asked, "What are you working on now?"

I told her I was writing a book on fear. With her encouragement, I went on to tell her how I had asked my television and radio audience to write me about whatever fears were keeping them from living with freedom and joy. The responses, I told the television interviewer, had really helped me feel the pulsebeat of fear in people today.

The woman picked up on my statement with intensity. I sensed more than the interest of a skilled interviewer. The look on her face betrayed her own battle with fear.

We got into one of the deepest conversations I've ever had during a live television interview. The woman seemed to lose all track of time as she pressed me to explain how to cope with fear. What had been planned as a five-minute interview went on for twenty-five minutes, using up the entire half-hour program. Other guests had to be held over for the next day's broadcast.

After we went off the air the director came into the studio. He was a bit upset by the television hostess's disregard for the time schedule.

"Didn't you see me signaling you?" he asked the woman. "I didn't know how I was going to get you off the air. I almost pulled the plug on you two."

"Sorry!" the woman responded, "We were probing the raw nerve in people today. It just couldn't be rushed. I guess our conversation really pushed my button!"

After the director and camera crew left, the woman and I sat in the studio for a long visit over a cup of coffee. Now off the air, she could be more personal. She confided her own brand of fear. Though she was a success, she was battling a gnawing insecurity about her future as a person and as a performer.

"Where is it all going?" she asked. "It's the nights that are hard. I wake up at three o'clock worried whether or not I can pull off another day's program. Will I fall flat on my face? I guess that's why I found our conversation on this morning's program so vital to me."

Here was a popular, admired performer who was filled with the same fears of really living almost everyone else feels. We had a deep conversation about how God could help her with her fear. I was surprised at how willing she was for me to pray for her before I left the studio.

The Fear Epidemic

Fear has reached epidemic proportions in America. It is contagious. We become infected by it and pass it on to others. Like a disease, fear saps our energy and robs us of joy in life.

Far from being the exclusive problem of the neurotic, fear cripples most Christians and often pervades our families, even our churches.

Franklin Delano Roosevelt recognized the destructive power of fear when he said, "The only thing we have to fear is fear itself." That's a memorable statement. Yet fearing fear does not help us conquer it. If that were all it took, you and I would have defeated fear long ago. Our fear about what fear does to us only tightens its grip.

Cheap advice and simplistic sermons don't help either. We've all been told we shouldn't fear, just as if all we had to do was to decide we weren't going to be fearful anymore. So we feel guilty, thinking that we could get over our fear if we just tried harder. As a result, our fear increases.

To put it bluntly, we can't take fear. Fear takes us. And a good deal of the time we feel helpless in controlling it.

We question with British novelist Joseph Conrad, "How does one kill fear, I wonder? How do you shoot a spectre through the heart, slash off its spectral head, take it by the spectral throat?"

That's what millions of people today want to know. What can we do with our fears?

We can begin by identifying them. It's important to realize that our fears come from four different but interconnected worlds.

Our Frightening Global World

Obviously, the simplest answer is to blame our fears on the frightening world in which we live. Just reading the front page of any day's newspaper is enough to give us a bad case of the jitters: The ever-present threat of nuclear annihilation of humankind, the virulence of cancer, the alarming spread of AIDS, the danger of terrorism and violence, the breakdown of moral integrity—these are only a few of the thousands of things that keep us agitated.

Many would echo A. E. Housman's sentiments:

> I, a stranger and afraid,
> in a world I never made.

Our Personal World

But not all our fears make the daily newspaper. Our personal world is filled with what we would consider more than our share of fear-producing people and distressing situations. What is it for you? Who or what in the immediate world around you causes you fear?

Our Inner World

Yet another world is a source of fear—it's our inner world of thought, emotion, memory, and imagination. That's where fear is nurtured and grown. We'll wage a losing battle with alarm over the world's problems and our immediate circumstances until our inner fears are overcome.

Fear is not *primarily* caused by the world around us, but comes from within us and then is attached to people and problems we face. Often what we think we fear in a particular situation is not what we really fear. Our outer fears are connected to much more profound fears inside us.

This inner world of fear has been a lifelong concern to me. Over the years, as I've tried to deal with my own fears and help others battle theirs, I've usually found that our surface fears are expanded and exaggerated by the unresolved fears inside us.

To explore this inner world, I simply asked people, "What fear inside you keeps you from living life to the fullest?"

The thousands of responses from my congregation and our greater television and radio congregation across the nation were revealing. By breaking them down into categories, I came up with a list of real troublemakers. The most disturbing fears included the fear caused by hurting memories, the fear of rejection, the fear of losing control, the fear of being inadequate, the fear of sickness and death, and the fear of the future.

An Even Deeper World of Fear

But the more I've thought about these inner fears, the more convinced I have become that they are connected to an even deeper world inside all of us. This is the realm of our most private self, known only to us and to God. It is there in the core of our innermost souls that the taproot of fear exists. From there our deepest fear sends out its roots into our thoughts, becomes focused on people and circumstances in our immediate world, and then is expressed in fearfulness in our reaction to the alarming problems in the world at large.

All our efforts to overcome our fears on the other three levels will fail until we experience healing in the depth of our souls. It's there in the secret place of our spirit that we need to receive profound love, the only lasting antidote to fear. And only God can love us as much as we need to be loved. Not just once, but daily, hour by hour, moment by moment.

The Idea of This Book

From this need came the idea for this book. Wouldn't it be great to have a twelve-step program for living without fear that begins with our deeper fear in our private world? Then we could confront the fears it produces in our personal world. After that we'd be able to face our fears in our interpersonal world and finally gain confidence to live with fearless freedom in the perplexed, broader world of our culture.

My hope is that after considering each of the twelve steps with me, you will want to review them at the beginning of each day and apply them often during frightening pressures and problems throughout each day. In a time of history dominated by fear, you and I can become part of a fearless minority. We can lead a counterculture campaign against our archenemy: fear.

With this background on the levels of fear we face and with this challenge before us, we are ready to take the first step in living without fear.

Step Number One: *My fear is really loneliness for God. Therefore, I will claim His promise to never leave or forsake me.*

Fear is loneliness for God. We were created to receive His love and love Him. And He has chosen and called us to live in an intimate relationship with Him. He is initiator of that relationship, constantly seeking us, pursuing us with relentless love.

Many of us have heard and read about God's grace all our lives, and yet we still battle with fear. Why is it so difficult for us to really believe in God's love?

The Shortest Sermon on Record

John Albrecht, an Episcopal priest in Lake Orion, Michigan, tried to help his congregation with the shortest sermon ever preached. He stood in his pulpit to preach. After a long pause, he said, "Love!" and sat down. A long period of silence followed.

The *Guinness Book of World Records* has entered it as the shortest sermon on record. Some of the members of Albrecht's church said it was his best sermon! It would be difficult to tie that record with a better word. Love says it all.

And yet, simply saying the word "love" does not make it real. I'm sure that some of the members of the congregation who heard that one-word sermon felt frustration. Others probably felt some guilt over their own lack of love for others, and then perhaps a realization of their lack of love for themselves. But if what I'm hearing from people today is representative, I think most of the congregation that day felt a deep surge of loneliness. My friend Les used to respond that way to constant reminders of God's love.

"Love? Whose love? God's?" he used to wonder. "If God loves me, why do I have all this trouble? Where is He when I need Him? Is He really in control? Then why don't I sense His presence? Perhaps He's like most people—big promises and little performance."

Les has had lots of disappointments with people through the years. His dad left him and his mother when he was twelve—just the time he needed a dad the most. Friends have really let him down. And the most shattering blow of all was when his wife left him. It was a long, lonely separation. And even though she's come back, Les can't really believe she's home to stay.

Abandonment

If I were to write the shortest chapter on a basic cause of fear I would just print the word "Abandonment." And if I really wanted to get extravagant with length, I'd add three more words and make it, "The Fear of Abandonment." That, too, might make the *Guinness Book of World Records.* But it would miss the mark.

For good reason. Most of us are not in touch with our feelings of being abandoned. And so, we'd probably ask, "What's that got to do with our battle with fear?" It's got plenty to do with it. Inside all of us there are conscious and buried memories of feelings of abandonment.

Some, like Les, lost one of their parents through divorce. A recent Harris poll (reflecting a revised method for computing the national divorce rate) shows us the grim picture of one out of every eight marriages ending in divorce. Over three-fourths of these couples had one or more children. And no matter how the divorce is explained to them, children usually feel guilty and rejected.

The Impact of Death

Other people who feel abandonment as adults lost one of their parents through death during their childhood. This loss levels a severe blow to a person's security, especially if the loss occurs during the early teen years.

I can remember standing with a fourteen-year-old boy named Bobby, looking down on his forty-five-year-old dad who had just been seized with a massive heart attack and died. The boy looked me in the eye and sobbed, "How can I ever trust anyone after this? What am I going to do without my dad?"

Bobby came to see me the other day. It's been twenty years since his dad died. He's a dynamic Christian businessman, but he did not become one without an anguishing struggle.

In our conversation he told me of the years of battling fear. He had felt abandoned by his dad and by God. All of the explanations of death and efforts to comfort Bobby at the time of his dad's death had not seemed to help him. He wanted his dad back!

It was only years later when he got in touch with his feelings and stopped blaming God that he could be open to hear about God's love.

Illness in the Family

Some people can trace their feelings of abandonment back to the prolonged illness of a parent.

That was Jenny's problem. Her mother suffered a long illness after she gave birth to Jenny's younger brother. Jenny was seven at the time and was not allowed to see her mother for several weeks. When she was permitted to go into her mother's sick room in their home, she was told not to touch her. Her mother did not embrace her for months afterward.

All through her adolescent years, Jenny was reminded that her mother was not well. Even when she just needed to talk, she was told that her mother was resting and should not be disturbed. Jenny felt abandoned by her mother even though they lived in the same house.

Ellen, a woman in her early thirties, had an even more difficult childhood. Her father's alcoholism taught her not to trust anyone. Her fear of abandonment was rooted in the memories of her father's unpredictable behavior and absence of nurturing love.

Even though Ellen had attended a Bible college and seminary, her relationship with God continued to be one of distance and discomfort. There always seemed to be a hollow echo when she called out to God.

"I figured that God was just like my dad," she said. "No matter how hard I tried to reach out to God, His arms always seemed to be a bit short." She went on to say, "I could never really bring myself to look at His face. I was terrified that I would see my own father's angry, scowling face."

In her mid-twenties Ellen could no longer outrun the emptiness that plagued her. Depression and despair eventually drove her to seek counseling. It was there that a loving counselor helped her to see how her father's alcoholism had affected her and how she had transferred her fears of abandonment onto the Lord. She was finally able to allow God to heal the deep wounds that had crippled her.

Lack of Love

Some people have suffered the suspicion that their parents really cared more for a brother or sister than for them. Others were damaged when their parents punished them for failures by withdrawing affection from them.

My friend Tommy, a sixty-year-old dental surgeon, felt that kind of emotional abandonment. He can still remember his mother threatening that she wouldn't be at home waiting for him when he came home from school unless he got to work and improved his grades. Tommy can't shake the memory of running home breathlessly, day after day, wondering if she had kept her threat.

Still other people remember broken relationships with family members that have never been healed. Estrangement has much the same emotional impact as abandonment.

Not All in the Family

But the sense of abandonment isn't limited to family relationships. We've all had the experience of losing a friend through conflict or unresolved hurts. Being criticized is painful, but being discarded and treated as though we no longer exist is infinitely worse. It disturbs our ability to trust in the future.

The disappointments of life often pile up and give us a discouraged feeling that we've got to face the struggle of life alone. "Who really cares?" many ask in their down times. And then a more disturbing question comes to mind, "Doesn't God know what's happening to me? He must have forgotten me!"

Superficial Answers

We've been conditioned by superficial Christian teaching to think that the only evidence of God's presence is a constant flow of material blessings and having things go smoothly.

Not so. We live in a messed-up world that has fallen from God's perfect plan and is filled with evil people in mutiny against Him. Others couldn't care less about Him, and still others are determined to run their own lives. It's also a world in which illness, aging, and death constantly remind us of our mortality.

God has allowed us to be free in this troubled world. We're not puppets; we're persons who can use their freedom to choose to love Him in response to His love in Christ and His constant care for us.

Jeff has made that choice and expresses it in a vivid way: "In response to the old question, 'How can we trust God in a world like this?' I simply say I couldn't live in a world like this without Him. When I think of all the tragic things He's kept from happening and the way He's used the bad things that have happened, I'm amazed. I can't imagine making it without Him."

The truth is that God has called us in the midst of this topsy-turvy world to belong to Him. He understands that our ability to trust Him has been battered down by the discouragements and disappointments of life. He knows the painful feelings of abandonment we've endured in the lack of acceptance and affirmation from others.

But He knows something else: He knows how to get through to His beloved people when problems make them wonder if He has turned on them. So, here's some really good news!

Fear Not!

The Lord's constant word to us is "Fear Not!" There are 366 "Fear Not!" verses in the Bible—one for every day of the year and an extra one for Leap Year! Most of the admonitions are followed by a firm assurance of the Lord's presence or a stirring reminder of an aspect of His nature—like His faithfulness, goodness, lovingkindness, or intervening power in times of need.

Three of these "Fear Not!" verses are particularly helpful in taking our first step to living without fear. They were spoken to people who felt abandoned in adversity and needed both the assurance and the experience of the Lord's presence and loving care.

The Lord Captivated the Captives

The first two of these "Fear Not!" verses are actually twin verses from Isaiah 41:10 and 13. They were spoken by the Lord through Isaiah to the Israelites held captive in exile. In verse 10, the Lord spoke directly to the people's discouraged sense of abandonment. "Fear not, for I am with you; be not dismayed, for I am your God. I will strengthen you, yes, I will help you, I will uphold you with my righteous right hand."

The Hebrew word for "fear" can also be translated "dread." "Don't dread life because of your circumstances," God seemed to say. "Don't be afraid of your unfamiliar surroundings here in exile away from the securities of Jerusalem and the temple. I am your God; and I am with you in spite of everything!"

The words "Do not be dismayed" in verse ten really mean "Don't look around furtively in panic," as if casting about for some other hope that would bring security or comfort. Looking only to God for help is not an easy task for anyone in any age. How could the people of Israel respond to that statement without the further promise God gave them: "I will uphold you with my righteous right hand"?

In Hebrew, the right hand of God is metaphorical for His presence and power. It is His hand that uplifts us when we are down, upholds us when we are weak, and uprouses us when we are sunk in cowardly lethargy.

But note, it's God's *righteous* right hand that takes hold of us in our fears. Here "righteous" means in keeping with God's character, consistent with His nature. The key word that expresses this for us is "grace": God's unlimited care and unqualified love. That's what we need when we feel separated from Him because we fear that He might have forgotten us. When our fears so dominate our thinking that we shy away from trusting even Him, He invades our self-devised solitary confinement and reveals Himself as our Friend.

How God does that is explained in verse thirteen, "For I, the Lord your God, will hold your right hand, saying to you, 'Fear not, I will help you.'"

Face to Face

Let's picture that. Suppose that the Lord Jesus extended His right hand to you. Naturally you'd respond by offering your right hand. In order to shake hands properly, the two of you would have to be face to face.

If you stood on His left side, you'd have to reach across Him to get His right hand; conversely, if you stood on His

right side, you'd have to reach across your own chest to
grasp His right hand.

Who'd ever shake the hand of a friend that way? No one.
Especially if we wanted to communicate something with
life-or-death intensity.

Instead of an awkward, impersonal side-by-side grasp of
our hand, the Lord takes hold of our right hand with His
righteous, grace-filled right hand. That puts us eye to eye
with Him. It's exactly what God intends. He has something
He wants to say to us that He wants us to hear with the ears
of our soul. He wants to get through to that deep inner place
in us where our fears fester.

"You don't need to be afraid," He says. "I am in charge of
your life. I will never leave or forsake you. Trust Me. Take
this first step to living without fear. I am Jehovah-Shammah,
the Lord is there. And wherever you are, be more sure of this
than you are of your next breath—I will be there."

Fear Not on the Stormy Seas of Life

The third "Fear Not!" verse I want to consider with you
was spoken by Jesus to the disciples when they were caught
in a raging, turbulent storm on the Sea of Galilee (John
6:15–21). They were terrified.

Storms on the Sea of Galilee are often violent. The strong
winds howl through the gorges in the mountains, which
act like wind tunnels, concentrating the blasts of gale on
the sea.

The disciples had ridden out many a storm on the sea. But
this was unlike any storm they had faced before. It lasted
nine hours. And during those dangerous hours, the disciples only rowed three or four of the six miles across the sea.

"If only Jesus were with us now!" they must have thought.
A few hours before, they had witnessed His miracle of the
feeding of the five thousand. He had retired to the moun-
tain, and the disciples had set off across the sea for Caper-

naum. "If the Master could do that with the loaves and fishes, He could save us now!"

Then Jesus came to them, walking on the angry sea. That He could come to them over the sea was enough reason for awe. But the words He spoke filled them with both wonder and worship. Above the howling of the wind and the surging of the sea, Jesus spoke with divine authority that rolled like thunder. "It is I; do not be afraid."

The Master then got into the disciples' boat and they immediately made it to the shore. The men never forgot those words. Nor can we.

The English translation of Jesus' fear-liberating words doesn't really do justice to the true meaning. In the Greek it is *Egō eimi mē phobeisthe.* I think this is one of Jesus' twenty-two "I AM" assertions. I like to translate it, "I AM; have no fear." In the Greek version of the Exodus passages of the Old Testament, *Egō eimi,* I AM, was used to translate God's name, *Yahweh.* When Jesus said, "Before Abraham was, I AM" (John 8:58), the same *Egō eimi* is used.

For me, the literal impact the words spoken to the disciples is, "Yahweh; have no fear." Jesus claimed to be none other than God with them, Immanuel.

The Calming of Our Storms

And Christ comes to you and me in our lonely fear with all power and authority. He will not leave us helpless in the restless seas of life.

Sometimes the Lord rides out the storm with us and other times He calms the restless sea around us. Most of all, He calms the storm inside us in our deepest inner soul. And when He does, we can begin to face all of the fears that disturb us in our thinking, in our personal relationships and responsibilities, and in our culture.

I experienced that peace when I first invited Christ to live in me in the spring of 1949. The following summer I went fishing in Canada with my dad. About that same time, he had renewed his faith in Christ. The Lord used our time together to bind us into a deeper relationship than we'd ever known.

While we were fishing, a storm came up and thrashed the lake into dangerous waves. We were tossed about like a cork on the lake. Our small fishing boat was nearly capsized.

Then, when we thought all hope of surviving was gone, suddenly the wind subsided, and in a few minutes the lake was flat as a mirror.

Dad and I looked at each other. Then he said quietly, "Lloyd, the Lord is here!" And indeed He was.

But I'm no less convinced that the Lord has been with me when the storms around me didn't cease. The sea He calms then is inside my soul. With that peace replacing our fears, we can take anything.

So *fear not!* You belong to the Lord and He will never abandon you.

Step 2 _____

I will overcome my crippling fears
with a creative fear of God expressed with
awe and wonder, adoration and faithful obedience.
He is the only Person I have to please.

_____

Children of a Looser God

EVERY SO OFTEN, I HAVE BREAKFAST WITH A GROUP OF WRITERS, managers, and performers from the entertainment community here in Hollywood.

The conversation around the breakfast table is fast-moving and filled with quips and stories. Each man tries to top the others' lines. The mixed bag of current events is opened and reviewed with humor, and there is lively armchair quarterbacking for everything from politics to religion.

You can imagine the field day the group had over the recent scandal concerning the morality and financial integrity of some media evangelists.

My good friend Johnny Grant, a popular television and radio host who is also an outstanding community leader and a committed Christian, got off a one-liner that's worth remembering. He worded a catchy twist on the title of a popular movie, *Children of a Lesser God*.

Johnny said, "The problem today is that too many Christians want to be 'Children of a Looser God'!"

That's not a bad analysis of some Christians in every age of history. In fact, there is a measure of that tendency in all of us. We want to pare down to our size the majesty and righteousness of God. His holiness and justice unsettle our easy ethics and challenge our fluctuating values. At times we'd all like both a lesser and a looser god. Sometimes we even create one.

The Frightening Loss of Awe and Wonder

As a result, there's a loss of awe and wonder in our relationship with the Lord God. We've dropped the bracing biblical phrase "the fear of the Lord" from our list of Christian virtues.

That's frightening. Literally. Terror grips us when we lose our fear of God. Without that one creative fear, we have no defense against all our destructive fears.

I'm not talking about a cringing anguish before an imperious tyrant God, but an awe and wonder that is expressed in adoration, praise, and *obedience*. The Holy God is our creator and judge as well as our redeemer and friend.

False Gods

Our reverence is misspent when it is squandered on anything or anyone other than the Lord God. Debilitating fear pervades our thoughts and feelings when we sneak around the first commandment, "You shall have no other gods before Me" (Exod. 20:3). Idolatry is giving to any person, purpose, or plan the ultimate allegiance and control that really belongs to God.

Unfortunately, we tend to elevate the things and people we fear to the status of false gods. When we fear certain people and need their approval too much, we seek to please and placate them as if they were the source of our worth. They become little gods in our lives.

The same can be true of our families, careers, money,

reputation, health, accomplishments of the past, or dreams for the future. Anything or anyone we cannot bear the thought of losing has become enthroned with God-like status in our lives.

That's a painful, disturbing thought. As uncomfortable as it may be, test it out. Reflect on what makes you afraid. Could it be that this very thing or person is competing with the Lord God for first place in your life? When we think about that, we want to pray with William Cowper:

> The dearest idol I have known,
> Whate'er that idol be;
> Help me to tear it from thy throne,
> And worship only thee.

Step Number Two

Our first step in living without fear was to trust that God will never leave or forsake us. His presence with us not only gives us comfort and courage but also leads us to a great challenge. God wants to claim our misdirected reverence and set us free to love and serve Him above all else. That leads us to our next step.

Step number two: *I will overcome my crippling fears with a creative fear of God expressed with awe and wonder, adoration and faithful obedience. He is the only Person I have to please.*

This second step may have startled you.

"Hold on!" you may be thinking. "First you quote God's words 'Fear not!' and now you tell us that we must fear Him. Doesn't that add one more panic to our fear-loaded hearts? Are we really to fear God? How can the Bible teach the 'fear of the Lord' and at the same time admonish us 'not to fear'?"

Consider the Context

In the Bible there's a distinction between dread and reverence. The problem is that often the same word is used for both. The most common Hebrew word for "fear," *yārē'*, signifies godly reverence, a lifestyle of obedience, or just plain human terror.

For example, in Genesis 15:1 God appears to Abram and says, "Do not be afraid [of Me]." In Deuteronomy 6:2, Moses tells the people that the commandments and provisions of God have been given "that you may fear the Lord your God." And the psalmist says, "Blessed is the man who fears the Lord" (Ps. 112:1). The same verb, *yārē'*, is used in all of these references.

In the Greek New Testament, *phobos* refers both to terror and dread and also to reverential fear. Jesus' command to the disciples to "Fear not!", which we considered in the previous chapter, uses a closely related word. *Phobos* is also used to describe the quality of reverence of the early church, "And walking in the fear of the Lord and in the comfort of the Holy Spirit, they were multiplied" (Acts 9:31). The word *deilia* is also used for "cowardly fear" (2 Tim. 1:7) and *eulabeia* for "holy fear" (Heb. 5:7; 12:28). But in the majority of cases *phobos* is employed to express both good and bad fear.

So in both the Old and New Testaments we must look at the context to discover which sort of fear we are encountering. The thrust of each passage will make clear whether it is constructive or debilitating fear that is meant.

Reverence That Leads to a Right Relationship

The important thing to discover is the crucial part that reverential awe plays in bringing us into a right relationship with our Holy God. It is in this relationship of complete trust and submission that we receive the power to overcome our fears. Without that relationship we will have to wage a lonely battle with fear on our own resources.

Solomon said, "The fear of the Lord is the beginning of knowledge" (Prov. 1:7). The Hebrew word for "beginning" can also be translated "choice part" or "chief part." And so we can paraphrase Solomon's words, "Awe, wonder, and humility are the choice, chief part of knowing God." Everything else flows from that healthy fear.

Different Reactions to the Fear of God

There are four possible reactions to the fear of God. The first three make us children of a looser or lesser god who is really no God at all. The fourth shows us how to be children of the true God. Let me explain and illustrate what I mean with the stories of four very different people. Many of us will identify with one of the first three. My prayer is that we'll all discover the liberating and creative fear experienced by the fourth.

An Overdose of the Dread of God

Some Christians have had an overdose of the wrong understanding of the fear of God. They cannot glorify or enjoy God because they have been taught to dread Him rather than adore and love Him with humble trust.

My friend Richard was raised in a legalistically religious family. He was taught to be afraid of God. In practical terms that meant he was conditioned to dread the wrath of an angry, judgmental God. And yet he was to try to please that God by following, to the letter, the rigid rules of his parents' brand of Christianity.

As a result of this childhood conditioning, Richard developed a very cautious attitude toward life. Richard cannot ever remember feeling God's love and forgiveness, and he finds it difficult to imagine ever being close to Him.

The upshot of all this is that my friend does not feel awe and wonder over the majesty and goodness of God, but rather a shrinking aversion that has only multiplied his fears.

Rejection and Rebellion

The second type of reaction to the fear of God is rebellion. It's the "Who needs this?" reaction.

Julie is a good example of this reaction. She had a background much like Richard's, but her response was quite different. She remembers that her parents kept her in line by threatening her with judgment and punishment from God. When she went away to college and got out of the grip of their control, she declared her independence from them and from the "cosmic policeman" god she had been taught to fear.

Because Julie never replaced the negative conditioning she received with a positive faith, she is filled with the floating sense of fear we talked about in the first chapter. She has an overactive conscience, but she has nowhere to turn in times of failure or in the demanding pressures of life.

Recently Julie said, "Lloyd, I'm afraid. Life is like a courtroom without a judge. There's no objectivity, no standard, no edge on which to cut. It's all dependent on me. I am left to decide what is right, and I'm not always sure. I feel lonesome and afraid.

"I don't want to go back to the religion of my parents with all that fear. I thought I was getting away from fear. But now I have more than ever."

Ignorance of the Fear of the Lord

By far the largest number of Christians today would fit into a third group. Unlike Richard and Julie, they've never had to wrestle with a misinterpretation of what it really means to fear the Lord. They've never heard much about it. The churches they attend seldom, if ever, mention it.

The emphasis of much of contemporary Christianity is on God's acceptance, with far too little teaching about our accountability to Him.

Dan was raised in that type of shallow Christianity. He believed in God and said his prayers, but his spiritual growth was stunted.

I met Dan at an executive leadership seminar where I spoke. In our conversations, I soon discovered why his faith was shallow. The god of his life was his career and his reverence was his passion for success.

The Stress of Success

Dan is part of the Yuppie generation. Like many of his peers, he achieved great success early in life and accumulated many of the Yuppie status symbols of that success. Yet his life was unsatisfying and joyless.

Los Angeles Times writer Betty Cuniberti aptly described the problem of people like Dan in an article headlined "Yuppie Angst—Coping with the Stress of Success."

"They are well stocked with MBAs, VCRs, and BMWs. But they are SAD," Cuniberti wrote. "Many of the most successful baby boomers find their jobs long on salary, short on satisfaction, a situation . . . that can lead to serious emotional problems. Their Victorian homes may be stuffed with high-tech gadgetry but the owners feel empty inside."[1]

Dan's emptiness was very real. It showed up in lots of fears. He was worried about failure and about not being able to keep up with his friends.

Dan was raised in a traditional Christian home. He was taught that God loved and cared for him. But he missed two important truths. First, he failed to understand that God had a plan for his life. Second, he failed to realize that he was responsible to Him for the use of his immense talents and intelligence.

For Dan, God was a sort of benevolent, permissive "Uncle Joe." He prayed to Him in times of need and expected help to accomplish his own plans and purposes. This big-league, christianized Yuppie's values and lifestyle were conditioned by culture and not by his faith. And yet, at thirty-five, Dan was wondering, "Is this all there is?"

George Bernard Shaw said, "There are two sources of unhappiness in life. One is not getting what you want; the other is getting it." Dan got what he thought he wanted, but in the process he almost closed himself off from the Father's judgment and healing.

A Healthy Fear of God

The fourth group of people are those who have a healthy experience of the fear of God. They don't swagger in His presence; they fall on their knees. They believe in a Holy God in whose presence they worship with wonder and praise over His power and greatness. They know that they could not come into His glorious presence except by His invitation. He is infinite, eternal, and unchangeable. He alone is God in His majesty, wisdom, goodness, justice, and truth. Only He can make the absolute demand for our obedience and provide the supernatural power to accomplish it according to His will.

God is also our judge.

In a culture dominated by children of a looser god, that truth may not win a popularity contest, but it must be said. We are accountable to our Father for what we do with what He has entrusted to us—our own lives, the lives of people around us, and the magnificent natural world in which He has etched His signature with grandeur.

The Positive Results of Healthy Fear of the Lord

Healthy fear of the Lord has very positive results. That's the promise the psalmist gives in one of my favorite verses about the fear of the Lord. "The secret of the Lord is with those who fear Him, and He will show them His covenant" (Ps. 25:14).

The Greek word for "secret" really means "friendship." Spurgeon said it implies "confidential intimacy and select fellowship."

What does God do when we come to Him with reverent fear? He welcomes us as friends and shows us His covenant. A covenant is a promise that establishes a relationship of mutual trust. The psalmist is speaking, of course, of the covenant the Lord made with Abraham and later confirmed to the nation of Israel, "I shall be your God and you shall be My people."

But we become the Lord's people under a new and better covenant. God comes to us in Christ, Immanuel, "God with us." He comes first in judgment and then in grace. He confronts us with what we are and then with what He has destined us to be. Again we respond with awe and wonder. He knows all about us!

The depth of God's love is revealed in this covenant. He reconciles us to Himself through Christ's death on the cross. When we experience the Father's wondrous love for us, we are filled with even greater awe than before. As Paul joyfully expressed it, "You did not receive the spirit of bondage again to fear [dread], but you received the Spirit of adoption by whom we cry out, 'Abba, Father'" (Rom. 8:15). No longer do we dread God but call Him by the most intimate of names. We rejoice with sheer astonishment over His glory and His reconciling love.

The New Dan

Earlier, I promised that I would illustrate this fourth group with the story of a person who has experienced this healthy fear of the Lord. You may be surprised that it's the story of Yuppie Dan.

A few paragraphs ago we left him trapped in his fears, urgently needing a genuine experience of the fear of the Lord. I'm thankful Dan's story didn't end there.

The essence of healthy fear of the Lord is humility. Dan's

real problem was that his lesser god was himself. No wonder he became fearful! With all his gifts he could accomplish almost anything with superb excellence. Except one thing: he couldn't be Lord over his own life.

It was when Dan realized how far he'd fallen short of God's plan for him that he was filled with holy fear. He saw how preoccupied he'd been with his self-serving lust for success.

With anguish he reviewed the way he'd used people as rungs in his arrogant climb up the ladder of success. Especially disturbing for him was the way he had hurt his lovely wife, whom he had treated like one of the many things he'd accumulated to fortify his image of accomplishment.

Added to this, Dan had been deeply moved by the witness of some dynamic Christian executives who had spoken during the seminar. They had shared how the Lord led them and their companies to become involved in community problems, human suffering, and world hunger.

Dan had to admit that he'd been living in his own little world while soul-sized issues swirled around him. He saw how irrelevant his life really was when compared to what God was up to in the world. Dan's pride was being broken by a holy fear. By that time he was ready to hear the Gospel of God's love in Christ with new ears.

All this led to one of the most moving commitments I have ever shared with another person. And the transformation is not over. One of the things I asked Dan to do was to spend fifteen minutes every morning reading the Bible and reflecting on the greatness and glory of God, and then report in for duty to serve Him.

In a recent conversation on the phone, Dan exclaimed, "Lloyd, what a puny God I had! It was like shutting myself up in a three-foot by seven-foot tall hut on the floor of the Grand Canyon. As God kicked in the door, blew off the roof, and knocked down the walls, I beheld His grandeur and glory." I've heard conversion described in lots of ways, but never as vividly as that.

Dan, a child of a looser god, has become a man of the Holy Lord God, and the same Lord God wants nothing less for you and me.

Many years ago writer and pastor James Fordyce shared the secret of how awe and wonder cures our sapping fears:

> Henceforth the majesty of God revere,
> Fear Him and you have nothing else to fear.

Step 3

I will face my fears, retrace them
to their source in my heart,
displace them by making my heart Christ's home,
and erase them with His perfect love.

A Gnawing
Uneasiness

'PAPA 'OYD!" MY THREE-YEAR-OLD GRANDDAUGHTER ERIN
squealed as she ran toward me and leaped into my out-
stretched arms. Her sister, Airley, one-and-a-half, was only
a few baby steps behind. I also swept her into my arms and
held the two of them with sheer delight and grandfatherly
gratitude.

"I love you!" I said, cuddling the girls.

"'Ov 'ou too!" Erin responded, hugging my neck.

I'm called by lots of names and titles. Lloyd, Lloyd John,
my nickname—Oggie, Pastor, and the more formal Dr.
Ogilvie. None of these, however, sounds the note of joy in
my ears and affection in my heart like Erin's rendition of
"Papa Lloyd."

It was a wonderful moment of tenderness. As I held the
two of them, I thought of how much I loved them. Then I
thought of God's love for them. If I multiplied my love
billions of times, I would only touch the edge of the immen-
sity of His love for my precious grandchildren.

The Pleasure of Our Father's Heart

Then it hit me. If my granddaughters can bring that much pleasure to me, is it possible that I bring pleasure to my heavenly Father's heart? Again I pondered the infinite, incalculable depth of His love and asked myself, "Can I run to God with the same childlike freedom and enthusiasm that Erin and Airley express when they run to me? Can I let go and allow Him to hold me with loving acceptance and assurance?"

Often we can't. Just thinking about the things we've said or done makes us feel unworthy. This causes us to feel that God should meet us with a stiff arm of judgment rather than with open arms of acceptance.

We project our own self-condemnation onto God.

When we need Him the most, we feel estranged. There is an uneasy distance between Him and us.

But when we feel this separation from God, who moved? Did God? No! We did! His love toward us has not changed, but our attitude toward Him has become strained and cautious. We feel an aching emptiness.

Unruly Tenant

It's then that our hearts become a landlord to an unruly tenant. Fear takes up residence and begins to act like it owns the house of our inner soul.

This fear is very different than the awe and wonder we talked about in the previous chapter. Rather, it is a cold dread, a feeling of discord and jangled unrest.

I am convinced that this deep, inner fear is the root of our lesser, external fears. It gets focused on frightening situations, alarming circumstances, and troublesome people. All our efforts to overcome our surface fears will be ineffective until this deepest fear is exposed and healed.

Getting to the Root of the Problem

The truth is—what we think we fear is usually not what we fear. One of the basic causes of fear is self-inflicted estrangement from God. We were created to know Him, experience His unqualified love, love Him in return, and enjoy an intimate fellowship with Him. If we never come to know Him, or if our relationship with Him has only been a vague religious belief in Him, or if we have drifted away from Him in willful independence—the gaping cavern in our souls will be filled with this most profound of all fears.

At its core, this basic fear is really a manifestation of guilt. It is the universal and inevitable human reaction to being separated from God.

You may be surprised that I've used the word guilt to describe that condition. Over the years, in deep conversations with people about their inner thoughts and feelings, I have discovered that many of them have a sense of incompleteness, as if they were created for something they haven't yet discovered or achieved. Unable to grasp a greater purpose in life, they feel out of sync. Something—they're not sure what—is wrong.

This floating sense that things are not quite right is the tug of God in our souls. No amount of human reassurance and affirmation seems to heal the unrest. Achievement and success cannot relieve the insecurity and anxiety. God is creating in us a longing for Himself, and the disjointed, fragmented sense of alienation will persist until we know His unconditional love and acceptance and discover His will for our lives.

This general floating sense of guilt is soon attached to our mistakes and failures. We end up feeling down on ourselves because of what we've done or said. That motivates the fear of judgment and punishment.

The Guiles of Guilt

The strange twist is that this guilt prompts many people to run from, rather than into, the accepting, reconciling arms of God. By refusing to submit to His judgment, we close ourselves off from His reconciling love, the only source of healing for fear.

A vicious circle results. Guilt causes us to fear punishment; we either condemn ourselves or begin self-justifying improvement programs; our guilt deepens as we become further alienated from God, starting the circle all over again.

Non-Christians are not the only people caught in the trap of guilt. Strange as it may seem, the inner sense of separation from God is felt by many who believe in Him. I meet them everywhere. They are church members, successful Christian businessmen and women, even pastors, and Christian leaders. And yet, they are unsure of God's unlimited grace for them.

The Plight of the Self-Righteous

My friend Tim is a good example. I met him and his wife, Jan, recently. Their story shows the plight of good people who are suddenly confronted with fear and discover that in spite of being religious they are alienated from God.

Tim was raised by good, moral parents. From early childhood he was taught to believe in God and to try to please Him. The way to do that, he was told, was to do what was "right." That "right" was interpreted to him in the rules and regulations his parents set down. He was praised when he measured up and punished when he failed.

God was established as the higher authority of his family's life. Prayers of gratitude for God's daily blessings were said at every meal. What Tim's parents did not have and, therefore, could not expose him to was an intimate relationship with God. They were self-reliant, responsible people who taught him to work hard and to use the talents God had given him.

Tim's parents were leaders in the church in his hometown. Tim was enrolled in the church school at an early age and was awarded the gold star for perfect attendance right through his teen years. He was confirmed at fourteen and became a leader in the Scout troop and youth fellowship.

The amazing thing is that Tim cannot remember ever being taught about how to know God personally. God's love was presented in His goodness and providential care. Tim believed that God would help him live out the clear moral integrity his parents had taught him. At no time was he confronted with the fact that, in spite of his model behavior, he was separated from God in the depth of his being.

After college, Tim's talents, excellent mind, and industriousness made him a sought-after employee. Soon he was given executive responsibility and was on his way to financial and social success. He married Jan, an outstanding woman who shared his values and goals. Together they pursued their successful careers.

You may have leaped ahead of the story and pictured some personal or professional crisis that brought Tim to a realization of his need for a profound experience of God's grace. Wrong. There were no tragedies, moral failures, or marital problems.

A Gnawing Uneasiness

God is wonderfully original in the way He works with each of us. For some, life must fall apart before we realize how much we need Him. It happened differently for Tim. At age forty, he became aware of a gnawing uneasiness. At first, he wrote it off as a mid-life crisis. He changed jobs, moved to Los Angeles, and got busy in community activities. Still he felt a "pit-in-the-stomach" turmoil.

One Friday evening, as Tim was sitting alone at his desk, a terrible fear gripped him that he could not shake. It triggered a feeling of dread. Though he had tried to do all of the right things, he felt wrong. An inescapable sense of guilt flooded him. *Why do I feel this way?* he wondered. *I believe in God and have tried to live a good life. What's wrong?* Later that evening, Tim shared his experience with his wife. She had felt some of the same anxiety, but had never told him. One word described her feelings: emptiness.

Amazing. Here were two successful people who were both feeling fear they had never confided with each other. But now that they had been honest to each other, what could they do about their mutual need? Take a trip? Redecorate their house? Find a new hobby?

I'm thankful that before they ran off in all directions seeking to fill their emptiness with new activities or possessions, God intervened.

The Turning Point

One Sunday morning, while having breakfast, Tim and Jan watched our television program. The message on that program, though taped weeks before, was perfectly timed by God for them.

I spoke about the plight of the good person who misses the full measure of God's love because of self-righteousness. Then I went on to talk about the joy of an intimate relationship with God through Christ. That was contrasted with the emptiness of good people who do all the right things but still are sinners needing to be reconciled with God. I felt compelled to explain that often the working of the Spirit of God produces a disquieting dissatisfaction with life, then anxiety, and finally a sense of fear.

The message was concluded with some clear steps on how we can admit our emptiness and accept God's unlimited love in Christ. I described how to surrender our fears to

Christ, ask Him to fill us with His Spirit, and commit our lives to Him.

When the program was over, Tim said to Jan, "How did that preacher know about us? The message was just for us!"

The following Sunday they attended our church. I met them and we had the first of several good visits together. And finally, both Tim and Jan made a commitment to Christ and asked to be filled with His Spirit.

There are millions of people like this couple inside and outside the church. They profess to be Christians and try to live a good life, but they are still estranged from the Lord in their deep inner hearts. There is little assurance of His love and acceptance. Their hearts are filled with insecurity and self-judgment. The resulting fear becomes focused on situations, people, and frightening possibilities.

The Secret

The Apostle John gives us the secret of overcoming this fear in his first epistle to the Christians in the Roman province of Asia Minor. Though they believed in God, many of them were waging a losing battle with fear.

They faced rejection because of their faith, the constant threat of persecution, and the demeaning influence of false teachers who undermined their trust in Christ's atoning death and empowering presence. This was coupled with the opposition of a godless, secular culture, and conflict with pagan religions. Added to these fears were the pressures and difficulties of daily living.

Like us, they tended to blame people and problems for their fears.

In one of the most concise and penetrating statements in Scripture, John showed them how their external fears were attached to a deeper fear. What he wrote to these first-century Christians can give twentieth-century Christians an understanding of the origin of fear. "There is no fear in love," John tells us, "but perfect love casts out fear, because fear involves torment. But he who fears has not been made perfect in love" (1 John 4:18).

The Cause of Fear

Let's consider John's insight about the cause of basic fear. "Fear involves torment," he says. The Greek word for fear used here and throughout this verse is *phobos*, meaning panic, dread, and terror. This root fear, according to John, is caused by torment. The Greek word is *kolasis*. It means punishment or discipline. The torment is our fear of impending judgment.

I believe that this fear is inherent in all human beings. It is called by many names—anxiety, nervousness, incompleteness, unfulfilledness, a floating sense of guilt. At base it is a fractured relationship with the God who made us for Himself. He pursues us, and the closer He presses on our soul, the more we feel our emptiness. It is a gift of grace.

More Than Half-Healed

God will not leave us half-healed, with a vague concept of His lovingkindness that does not penetrate to our inner guilt. He knows the plight of the "good" Christian who talks about His love and still lives in what Thoreau called the "quiet desperation" of guilt-induced, hidden fear. He breaks through the barrier of the protective, partial truth that He loves us just "as we are." His love for us "as we are" also includes healing the guilt that has made us the fearful people we are.

John gives us a potent five-word prescription for receiving God's love for the healing of this fear in our innermost souls. "Perfect love casts out fear."

We've heard and seen these five words often. They are repeated frequently in worship services. We see them printed on posters and arranged calligraphically in greeting cards. We get a warm feeling of assurance when we hear or see them. They seem to hold out a wonderful promise if we could only grasp it.

But merely saying these words doesn't remove our fears. Some people find that the promise actually adds to their insecurity. Perfect love? Who can achieve that? And others wonder what the promise really means.

Does the knowledge that we are loved really eradicate our fears? If so, why are so many people who have heard about God's love still filled with fear? And what's more, why do those who have experienced His gracious provision and care continue to wrestle with distressing fears?

I think it is because most of us have misunderstood the true meaning of the word "perfect."

Perfect Love

The Greek word for "perfect," *teleios*, describes that which has reached its end, has accomplished its purpose, and is completed, fully grown, and mature. With this definition in mind, we then understand that God's love for us accomplishes its purpose when it heals our guilt, gives us the certainty of our security in Christ, and fills us with a complete confidence that we have been accepted in spite of what we've been, said, or done.

We experience God's perfect love in what He did and does through Christ. He came to humankind when we could no longer come to Him because of the alienation caused by guilt.

Christ was and is God's love accomplishing its goal: the reconciliation of His fearful children to Himself. The Master taught, modeled, and revealed the loving heart of the Father. And then, as the Savior of the world, He went to the cross to suffer not just for our *sins*, but for our *sin:* the guilt-motivated refusal to be loved and to love the Father in return.

On the cross, Christ endured not only the excruciating physical pain of the crucifixion, but the incalculable anguish of being separated from God. He took our guilt onto Himself. And there, during those hours on the cross, He received the full impact of the judgment of God. As the Lamb of God was nailed to that cruel cross, He was thinking of you and me as well as His executioners. "Father, forgive them; for they know not what they do" (Luke 23:34, KJV). The Roman soldiers didn't realize they were participants in the event that could free humankind from the penalty of sin. Nor do we when we harbor guilt and fear as if Jesus had never died.

At high noon on that tragic Friday darkness enshrouded Golgotha. For the three longest hours in history, Jesus suffered estrangement from the Father. As Paul put it, "He made Him who knew no sin to be sin for us, that we might become the righteousness of God in Him" (2 Cor. 5:21). That was God's purpose—to make us right with Himself. When those hours of darkness were finished, Christ sobbed out the reality of what He had been through. "My God, My God, why have You forsaken Me?" (Mark 15:34). The sacrifice of His life was the beginning of a new creation.

No wonder He shouted in triumph, "It is finished!" Indeed it was. It was complete, never to be repeated again. Perfect, for then, for now, and forever. And it's for you and me.

Verdict: Not Guilty

With the authority of God and the credentials of His cross, Jesus Christ pronounces us not guilty. He takes away our guilt for what we've been as well as what we've done. Graciously, He gives us the gift of faith to accept His forgiveness and be set free from our fear. John was right, fear has to do with torment. But Christ, perfect love Himself, casts it out.

Love and fear cannot coexist together. As John explained,

he who fears has not been made perfect in love. Unresolved guilt is still the breeding ground of fear within us. But the good news is that Christ never lets up on us until we are liberated.

When we invite Him to live in us, He, as perfect love, displaces our fear. Daily, moment by moment, within our hearts, He washes away our feelings of guilt and dislodges our fear. He stands guard at the entrance of our hearts with a "no-vacancy" sign in His hand. It is His plan and goal to constantly evict that unruly tenant, fear, from our hearts and continue to occupy them with His own presence.

Between Tenants

Most of us would probably have to admit that we're in the process of evicting the unruly tenant of fear. We know love can't be a roommate with fear. That's why we need our next step in our twelve steps to living without fear.

The first two steps we have taken in our conquest of fear prepare us for this next one. When we know that the Lord will never leave or forsake us, and that He will not take second place to our lesser gods, we are ready to confront our need for Him to remove our guilt-oriented fear.

Step number three is designed to help us do that. Here it is: *I will face my fears, retrace them to their source in my heart, displace them by making my heart Christ's home, and erase them with His perfect love.*

Face It

Face your fears, don't submerge them.

There are two undeniable things about our fears. They are real to us, and they won't go away simply by wishing them away. So we ask, "What is it in my life that causes me to fear? What makes me feel insecurity, alarm, or uncertainty?"

I find that my external fears all fall into one or more of

the following categories. Each one begins with the letter *P*: People, problems, perplexities, possibilities. How does that square with your experience? Whatever it is, step up to it and look it squarely in the eye.

Retrace It

Next, retrace your fears—refocus on your mind's eye the source of your present fears. What deeper anxiety lurks behind the present situation, circumstance, or relationship that is making you fearful? Is it some person who injured us or some past failure that is causing us to fear the future? Remember, if we don't deal with our past, we will compulsively repeat it.

In retracing our fears it is important for us to remember that what we think we fear is usually not what we fear. Most of our external fears are rooted in our deeper guilt-motivated fear that is the result of alienation from God. We have gnawing feelings of guilt not just because of things we've done, but because we willfully avoid intimacy with the Lord.

Displace It

After facing and retracing our fears, the next step is to ask Christ to move in and live in our hearts. This opens the way for Him to have His way in our hearts.

We can't evict fear on our own—only Christ can do that. The secret is to focus on Him and not on our fears. In doing that we will deliberately refuse to spend time rehearsing our fears.

My friend Terry Teykl expressed it this way, "Fear is the dark room in which we develop our negatives of frightening possibilities." But when we allow the Lord to flood our dark rooms with the brilliant light of His presence, our fears are dispelled completely. Instead, we will picture ourselves as the person Christ wants us to be.

Erase It

Finally, only Christ can erase our fears. It's His miracle. Our part is to pray, "Lord, I don't want this fear any more. I don't want to hang onto it as a false security any longer. I ask you to erase it and clean it off the blackboard of my memory."

How the Lord answers that prayer is the exciting thing I want to share in the next chapter about the healing of memories.

Step 4

I will let go of my hurting memories
of the past. I will not anticipate
the repetition of the past pain;
I will accept forgiveness from the Lord
and will forgive everything and everyone
in the past—including myself.

Left Luggage

GREAT BRITAIN'S RAILWAY STATIONS, AIRPORTS, AND HOTELS have places called "Left Luggage." They are exactly what the words imply—a designated area to leave luggage for a time.

I was reminded of this unique "left luggage" term this past summer when I was spending study leave in Scotland. After a time of concentrated study in my hide-away hotel, I decided to interrupt my work for a few days of fishing. All I would need for that brief interlude was some warm clothing and my fishing equipment. But since I would be giving up my room while I was away, the rest of my clothing, as well as my books and papers, had to be packed in a trunk.

When I was ready to leave, I called Jimmie, the old hall porter, and asked him to check the trunk in the hotel's "Left Luggage." When Jimmie arrived at my door to get the trunk, he wanted to know where I was going, how long I would be gone, and whether I intended to come back for my trunk. Then he said, "We've had guests who've had their 'left luggage' here for months. And some of them never pick it up."

I assured Jimmie that I'd be away for only a few days and that I really needed to forget about the unfinished work in the trunk for awhile. He completely missed my point. His parting reminder was, "Mind you, don't forget your left luggage!"

Jimmie's reminder not to forget my left luggage came back to my mind all too often while I was trying to catch an elusive salmon in the Dee River. In fact, worry over the work I had left behind kept me from enjoying the fishing. Finally, I said to myself, "The Lord has given you these few days to rest and relax. Now forget the left luggage!"

Reflecting on that experience makes me think about the place in our memories that might be called "left luggage." It's filled with the troublesome memories we wish we could forget. Instead of resolving them, we simply store them away. They are still there to haunt us. They cripple us from moving on into the future with freedom.

Upon boarding oceangoing ships, passengers' cases and trunks containing items not needed during the time on board are tagged, "Not needed for the voyage." Just so, many of our memories of the past are unnecessary for our voyage into a future of freedom. Especially we do not need the memories that remind us of our failures or of things others have said and done to hurt us.

Forgetting to Remember and Remembering to Forget

All too often, our problem is that we remember what we'd like to forget and forget what we need to remember.

For example, I remember a time I forgot something very important. When I was a pastor in Bethlehem, Pennsylvania, I had a small study in the basement of our home. One night I was burning the midnight oil. My concentration was interrupted by a gentle knock at the door of the study. There, attired in purple loveliness (which I will not describe in full detail!), stood my wife, Mary Jane. She held a little present in her hand, beautifully wrapped in purple paper (her favorite color) with a purple bow and purple note. With a beaming smile on her face, she handed it to me. I opened the note and read the words written in—you guessed it—purple ink: "Happy Anniversary. I love you." I had completely forgotten!

I've been known to forget other important things. One Saturday afternoon a call from the wedding hostess reminded me of a wedding half an hour away and saved my reputation.

I pride myself in preaching without notes. I'm thankful for a good memory. Even so, I've forgotten carefully memorized paragraphs of manuscripts and have finished repeating a poem with words and meter the poet would not have recognized! When that happens, I usually work all the harder to develop an accurate memory.

But I have to admit there are also times when I wish my memory were not so accurate. Like everyone, I keep some items in my "left luggage" that I need to forget. All of us have some memories we hope will never be exposed. Unfortunately, these skeletons rattle in the recesses of our minds and remind us that we have not forgotten. Added to those memories are the recollections of how others have failed us and the painful experiences of life we've endured.

Holding On to the Past

One of the greatest causes of fear in our lives is holding on to the past. The panic over being discovered for what we've been, combined with memories of hurts from others, produces a feeling of uneasiness about the past and a fear of the future.

This brings us to the next liberating step we must take in living without fear. It's easier to state than to take. But we can't do it alone. The Lord will help us.

Remember, in our pilgrimage together we're counter-culture Christians in a conquest against debilitating fear. The Lord wants us to conquer this fear of the past so that we can be free to live in the present and reach out to others who are still in bondage. He takes us by the hand as we consider, and then take, step number four: *I will let go of my hurting memories of the past. I will not anticipate the repetition of past pain; I will accept forgiveness from the Lord and will forgive everything and everyone in the past—including myself.*

God Forgives and Forgets

We will be able to take this momentous step if we consider another glorious aspect of God's nature—His memory and His ability to forget. One of His great attributes is that He deliberately forgets our failures but never forgets about us. That's so astounding, I hasten to assure you that it's not my idea but God's own revelation about Himself in the Bible.

In Isaiah 43, the Lord tells us what not to remember and why. He says, "Do not remember the former things, nor consider the things of old. Behold, I will do a new thing. Now it shall spring forth; shall you not know it?" (vv. 18–19). And why should we forget the old things? The Lord says, "I, even I, am He who blots out your transgressions for My Own sake; and I will not remember your sins. Put Me in remembrance; let us contend together; state your case, that you be acquitted" (vv. 25–26).

We are to forget the past by remembering the Lord. We are to remember He has forgotten our sins and failures. And yet, we must confess them specifically if we are to be healed. At His command we are to march through the prison of our memories, leading out each captive memory for display before Him. We are urged to state our own case against ourselves and then be acquitted. All of our mistakes and all the injustices that have wounded us must be brought into the court of His presence. Then as we finish our condemnatory judgment on ourselves and others He says, "I forgot that long ago; now you are free to forget it."

No one can take grace lightly. God's promise to forget has been sealed with the blood of the Cross. Throughout the Old Testament, His repeated assurances "I will remember your sins no more," not only express His forgiving-forgetting heart, but also look forward to Calvary. When Christ died for us, He forgave our sins and freed us once and for all from slavery to destructive memories.

An Example of the Art of Forgetting

Perhaps among all of our Old Testament spiritual ancestors, the most vivid illustration we have of the importance of forgetting destructive events from the past is Joseph. In fact, so important was the needed to forget that Joseph actually named one of his sons Manasseh, which means, "The Lord has made me to forget."

Without doubt Joseph had a good many experiences in his past that he needed to forget—and forgive, too. In the biblical account of his life we first meet him as a lad of seventeen in Canaan. He was the favorite son of his father, Jacob. Out of jealousy, his brothers rejected him, tried to do away with him, and finally sold him into slavery in Egypt. There he rose to power in the household of Potiphar, the captain of Pharaoh's bodyguards. When Joseph rejected the sexual advances of Potiphar's wife, she lashed out at him in anger and accused him of trying to rape her. Joseph's refusal to compromise his moral and spiritual integrity landed him in prison. But God was with him.

Without rehashing here all of the drama in Joseph's prison experience, I'll simply remind you of his relationship with Pharaoh's butler and baker. They had, as you remember, displeased the Pharaoh and had been turned over to the captain of the guard where Joseph was incarcerated.

Then when the butler and the baker each had a dream, Joseph, with the Lord's help, told them what their dreams meant.

Much later, Pharaoh's butler, who had been released and restored to his official position, remembered Joseph's gift for interpreting dreams. He recommended him to Pharaoh who had experienced two very puzzling dreams. Once again the Lord acted through young Joseph and gave him the meaning of Pharaoh's dreams.

In interpreting the dream, Joseph explained to Egypt's ruler that they would experience seven prosperous years of lush crops. This period would then be followed by seven years of drought and famine. Then, having interpreted the dreams, Joseph gave Pharaoh advice on what to do and how to prepare for what was to happen. Pharaoh was so impressed by Joseph's wisdom that he made him prime minister and vice-regent over all of Egypt.

Things turned out exactly the way Joseph had predicted. And for seven years, under his leadership, they stockpiled surplus grain for the future. Then famine paralyzed Egypt and the surrounding near Eastern countries.

Back in Canaan, Joseph's father and brothers ran out of food. Their situation became so intense that Jacob sent his sons to Egypt to buy supplies. Since Joseph was in charge of distributing food supplies, it was inevitable that he and his brothers would meet. Joseph recognized them, but they didn't know him.

Next follows the fascinating story of Joseph's cat-and-mouse game with his brothers until he finally told them who he was and that he held no grudge against them. And so this particular scene in the drama ends with Joseph, his father, and his brothers all being united again. With the Lord's help, Joseph was able to forgive his brothers and forget the evil they had done him. And because he did, they all settled in Egypt and the Hebrew nation was born.

Now, if we are to forgive ourselves we need to assume the

name Manasseh, "The Lord has made me to forget." We also need to discover how to cooperate with the Lord in the dynamic process. He will not force us against our wills. The burning question is how can we become willing participants? How does the healing of memories take place?

Troublesome Memories

Here's how it has worked for me. Several years ago, I realized the "left luggage" room of my memory was overloaded with three kinds of troublesome memories. First, there were memories I hoped would never be exposed; second, there were hoarded memories of failures; and, third, there were hurting memories of what others had done to me. Repeatedly, I would go into my "left luggage" room, unpack those memories, and rehearse them. I found that all the pain was reexperienced. A lot of energy was squandered in this unproductive habit. It blocked my ability to remember the good things.

One day I decided I needed to receive the Lord's healing. I wanted to be free to live in the present and be hopeful about the future. I took an 8 1/2 × 14 inch sheet of paper and made a long list of the memories I needed to forget. Three headings divided the memories into categories: Secret Memories; Memories of My Failures; and Memories of What Others Have Done.

As I worked, I asked the Lord to help me dredge up anything that I had consciously or unconsciously buried. Because I had not brought things before Him on a daily basis, the list was long, covering several years. It was hard, sometimes painful, work.

When the list was as complete as I could make it by being honest with myself and the Lord, I took each memory separately, went back over the event, and made a specific surrender of the memory to the Lord, claiming His forgiveness and healing. In the case of the list of hurts from others, I asked

for the power to forgive. Then in a special time of commitment to the Lord that I would remember to forget, I burned
the list. As the flames consumed the list, I sang Charles
Wesley's hymn, "O for a Thousand Tongues to Sing":

> Jesus, the name that charms our fears,
> That bids our sorrows cease,
> 'Tis music in the sinner's ears,
> 'Tis life, and health, and peace.
>
> He breaks the power of canceled sin,
> He sets the prisoner free;
> His blood can make the foulest clean,
> His blood availed for me.

Wesley's words about Christ's wanting to break the
power of canceled sin had special meaning for me. Two
thousand years ago, Christ had died on the cross for my
failures. But what I experienced now was the breaking of
the binding power of what He had already forgiven. That
happened when I claimed His healing power for each specific memory on my list.

This decisive turning point in my Christian life happened
after I had been a struggling disciple for several years.
Since then I've learned how important it is to keep "short
accounts"—that is, pay my bills promptly—with the Lord.
The memory liabilities side of the ledger needs to be cleared
each day.

But I don't always know what needs to be confessed,
cleared, and forgiven. Like all of us, I have a tendency to
hurry through the confession portion of my daily prayers
with a sweeping, "Lord, forgive me for all my failures and
mistakes." I need to be reminded often that the biblical
word for "confession" in the New Testament actually means
to "say the same thing after," to "give assent or agreement."
For me, that means allowing the Lord to tell me what needs
to be cleansed. Then I repeat after Him what He has exposed that needs forgiveness or healing on a daily basis

before it gets stored away in my mind to trouble me in the future. The simple daily prayer "Lord, show me what I need to confess" works wonders. It provides a consistent cleansing of mistakes I might defensively rationalize only to find that they haunt me later.

We Become What We Remember

Keeping short accounts with the Lord is so crucial because *we become what we remember.* Unresolved guilt, unconfessed failures, and unforgiven injuries from others make us fearful and cautious. Our obsession with negative memories short-circuits positive memories and causes us to forget God's goodness in the past—how He enabled us to face and overcome previous difficulties.

Recently, my wife and I celebrated our wedding anniversary with a dinner at a favorite restaurant. Our conversation focused on what each of us considered to be our twelve best memories of our years together. As we remembered, we laughed and cried. It was impossible to limit our lists to only twelve memories. One good memory sparked another. We reminisced late into the night and were the last people to leave the restaurant.

The remarkable thing about that conversation was the positive impact it had on our attitude toward our present life together. We were overcome with gratitude for the blessings God had poured out over the years. That gave us new gusto for the present challenges we face. I shudder to think what would have happened if we had tried to remember the twelve most hurting memories of times we'd failed each other. Thank God, those were not lurking in our minds to cloud our good memories.

We've learned the hard way that we are what we remember, both individually and together in our marriage. Whenever we harbor hurts we lock each other in the prison of the past. Inadvertently, we repeat the mistakes that are dominating our memories. Likewise, keeping short accounts with each other as well as with the Lord frees us to resolve difficulties quickly. With a liberated memory, we are able to focus on our blessings; rather than compulsively repeating the mistakes, we can expect a repetition of the positive memories.

Remember!

It's amazing how often the Bible challenges us to remember the faithfulness of God. In the Old Testament Israel is admonished repeatedly, "Remember your God!" And as we go over the history of the acts of God in Israel's life, we are filled with awe over what He did. Remembering God's great deeds we have new confidence about what He will do in our lives today. The psalmist's challenge to his own soul is a good reminder for us to give ourselves, "Bless the Lord, O my soul; and all that is within me, bless His holy name! Bless the Lord, O my soul, and forget not all His benefits . . . " (Ps. 103:1–2). He goes on in this stirring psalm to remember the Lord's forgiveness, healing, interventions, faithfulness, mercy, and strength in times of weakness. We, like the psalmist, have so much to remember about the consistent goodness of God.

In the Gospel account Jesus told His disciples—and us—"Do this in remembrance of Me." We're prone to limit this to the celebration of the Lord's Supper. But I believe Jesus' words go beyond that to include remembering what He has done for us in His death and resurrection. We are to act in remembrance of Jesus in all of life.

"Remember Jesus Christ!" was Paul's watchword. Because he did, his memories of past sins and failures were wiped out and his expectation of continued blessing was energized. The Apostle could face his problems because he remembered Jesus Christ. Just before his death Paul wrote to Timothy, "Remember that Jesus Christ, of the seed of David, was raised from the dead according to my gospel, for which I suffer trouble . . . even to the point of chains; but the word of God is not chained. Therefore I endure all things for the sake of the elect, that they also may obtain the salvation which is in Christ Jesus with eternal glory" (2 Tim. 2:8–10).

Paul's phrase, "according to my gospel," leaps out of these verses. Each of us has a gospel—the Good News of Christ according to our experience. It's the account of what His cross means to us and a record of what He has done in our own personal lives. The objective truth of the biblical Gospel, plus our own gospel, gives us the courage to be honest about what still needs to be healed in our memories. Knowing that Christ has forgiven us must be coupled with our forgiveness of ourselves and others. Does your gospel include how the Lord has healed and continues to heal your memory through the power of forgiveness?

The poet George Kenyon was depending on God's healing of his hurting memories when he wrote,

Lord, make me deaf, and dumb, and blind
To all "those things which are behind."
Dead to the voice that memory brings,
Accusing me of many things.
Dumb to the things my tongue could speak,
Reminding me of when I was weak.
Blind to the things I still might see,
When they come back to trouble me.
Help me press on to Thy high calling,
In Christ who keepeth me from falling.
Forgetting all that lies behind—
Lord, make me deaf and dumb and blind.
Like Paul, I then shall win the race
I would have lost but for Thy grace!

Forgiving Ourselves

Recently, at a Christian leaders' conference, I talked to a highly respected layman whose gospel did not include the dynamic of forgiveness of himself. He confided that he had been unfaithful to his wife and shared with me the painful remorse he felt over what he had done. The man was most fearful of being discovered. Though he had asked God to forgive him, he still feared that his reputation would be destroyed if the affair ever became public. That was unlikely. His wife had forgiven him and was not about to publish his failure. The woman with whom he'd been involved had married another man and moved to another community. Yet this man was in a panic.

"When did this affair occur?" I asked. I was astonished when he said, "Twelve years ago." Think of it! Twelve years of anxious days and restless nights. All because the final link in the experience of the perfect love which casts out fear had not been completed. The man had refused to forgive himself and had endured twelve years of self-inflicted torture.

But before we become too critical of this man, we need to reflect on what still lurks in our memories that needs our forgiveness. It may be more or less serious than his infidelity. The important thing is that we accept forgiveness— God's and our own. Then, if there is any restitution we need to make by asking anyone else's forgiveness, we must do it immediately.

Today's Actions Are Tomorrow's Memories

Since today's actions become tomorrow's memories, it's essential to take an incisive inventory of our present life. Is there anything we must hide? Is there anything we are doing that could not stand the test of absolute honesty or moral purity? If so, we can be sure it will be added to the composite of memories that will plague us with an even greater fear of having our past exposed.

My good friend Milton Brock, an outstanding Christian businessman, told me of a decision he made years ago.

Every decision and involvement had to withstand this crucial test: Would he have the slightest concern if his actions
were reported on the front page of the *Los Angeles Times*?
Not a bad test for evaluating whether what we do and say
today will be a good or bad memory a year from now.

Today can be the first day of building a new past. A
friend of mine named Mary discovered that five years ago.
In response to a sermon I'd given on the healing of memories, she came to see me to talk about her anxiety over the
past. Though Mary had been a Christian for years, she
carried the memories of a painful childhood, a divorce
years before that she had kept hidden from her friends, and
other mistakes she had made through the years. Struggling
to keep all this hidden, she was filled with fear. Her polished exterior portrayed a happy Christian. Inside, she was
a bundle of tension. Most of all she felt panic about the
future, being terrified that it would hold nothing more than
a repetition of the past.

After Mary had finished a long explanation of her deepest feelings, we talked about the power of forgiveness in
the healing of memories. I told her how the Lord's perfect
love casts out fear. I shared my own and others' experiences of forgiveness and the freedom to forgive. We talked
specifically about her failures for which she needed forgiveness and people she needed to forgive. I repeated
Christ's awesome promise in Revelation 3:20, "Behold, I
stand at the door and knock. If anyone hears my voice and
opens the door, I will come in to him and dine with him
and he with Me."

"Mary," I said, "will you open the door and invite the
Lord to fill you with His Spirit and heal your memories?"

"Yes," Mary replied with tears streaming down her face.
"I can't go on the way I am."

After we had had a long time of prayer together, Mary
opened the door of her memory to the Lord and committed
each one of her hurting, hidden memories to Him. At the

end of our prayers Mary told me she felt more at peace than ever before. Her face was radiant with joy.

I saw Mary the other day. "How are you doing with those memories?" I asked.

"Lloyd," she said, "the gnawing fear is gone! The pain has been totally removed from those memories. In fact, it's difficult to remember some of those haunting memories. And no longer having to hide my past has made me sensitive to other women who are suffering from the same kind of unhealed memories. It's especially exciting to be able to tell them what the Lord can do. What great memories I have of these past five years!"

The Lord who healed Mary stands at the door of all of our memories and knocks persistently. He wants to enter our left luggage room and tag all those hurting, hidden memories: "Healed—no longer needed for the voyage!"

Step 5 ___

Fear is estrangement from myself.
What I fear in others
I first fear in myself.
Therefore, in response
to God's unqualified acceptance,
I will embrace myself as worthy
of my own affirmation
and encouragement.

___

Embrace Yourself

It looks like a credit card. Same size, same plastic material. But it's probably more important for living without fear than any other credit card you own. And you'll not want to leave home without it!

It's called the Hug Card. At the center there's a black square. When you hold your thumb on the square for ten seconds, you'll discover how many hugs you need. If it remains black, you need four hugs; if it turns red, you need two hugs; green indicates you need only one hug; and if it registers blue, you are ready to give a hug away to someone else.

I've had lots of fun with my family and close friends, experimenting with the Hug Card. It's a great conversation piece, and I'm especially delighted when the black square turns to blue and I get to give a hug away.

Telling you about that card may seem like a lightweight beginning to a chapter in a book on the heavyweight subject of living without fear. Not at all. We all need hugs of affirmation and affection. And more than that, we need the embrace of total acceptance.

The One Person We Need to Embrace

As I've reflected on this idea, I've come to see that we not only need the embrace of acceptance and approval from others, we are in desperate need of being able to embrace *ourselves*. But because we know so well the real person inside our own skins, most of us have that haunting feeling that we don't deserve a hug from ourselves. Our sense of self-appreciation and self-esteem is low because we don't think we measure up.

And because we're convinced down deep inside that we're not very nice or that we are failures, we tend to be critical of ourselves. Even as we withhold approval from someone else we disagree with or dislike, we're unable to affirm ourselves, because we're sure we don't deserve it.

Instead of being "our own best friend" we become victims of a subtle but paralyzing kind of fear—fear of ourselves. No one knows our shortcomings and overlooks our struggles better than we do. We're fearful of our need always to be right, of our feelings of jealousy when a friend or colleague makes good, of our drive for prestige and power, or of our need to manipulate others to get what we want.

The other day I greeted a friend with a cheery "How are you?" He responded with surprising frankness. "I'll be okay if I can just keep Jack caged up!" Knowing Jack, I'm sure there are some great things in him that are being caged along with those things he fears about himself.

Most of us identify with Jack. Our past mistakes make us fearful about what we might do or say under pressure. Our "foot in mouth" disease has us constantly upset and in trouble. "How could I have said that?" pops out for most of us after a catty or heated exchange. And more than once at the end of a day I've said, "Self, I warned you never to act that way, but you've gone and done it again."

The Friend Inside

If we treated our friends the way we treat ourselves, putting down strengths and touting mistakes, we wouldn't have any friends left. And that's what happens when we get down on the person inside us. We risk losing one of the best friends we could ever have.

Abraham Lincoln said, "When I lay down the reins of this administration I want to have one friend left. And that friend is inside myself."

That's a tall order. A true friend knows our strengths and helps us develop them. He also knows our weaknesses and gives us courage to face and overcome them. He is not afraid of us. That's the kind of friend we have in Jesus Christ. And I firmly believe He is anxious to help us be the same kind of friend to ourselves that He is.

Think of it this way. In the third step to living without fear we claimed the biblical truth that perfect love casts out fear. Freed from guilt, we ran joyfully into the loving arms of the Father. Then, as we considered the story of Joseph, we asked God to heal the bitter memories that divide us from other people. Now we must grapple with how God's perfect love is worked out in our relationship with ourselves.

The Lord wants our love for ourselves to reflect His unconditional love. His love must heal our basic fear of ourselves. We are made in such a way that we are not truly free until we are willing to embrace ourselves as loved, cherished, and forgiven people with great potential. We need deliverance from the imprisonment we've inflicted on ourselves.

And so we must press on to the next vital step in living without fear. Step number five: *Fear is estrangement from myself. What I fear in others I first fear in myself. Therefore, in*

response to God's unqualified acceptance, I will embrace myself
as worthy of my own affirmation and encouragement.

Now, to explain this step, I want to share a moving experience I had while writing this book.

A Step I Needed to Take

Most writers write about what they want to learn and experience themselves. That was certainly true for me in writing this book.

My preparation involved me in a prolonged research into the causes and cures of fear. I carefully reviewed the observations I had collected in over thirty years of talking with people about their fears. But my study of fear has also included a ruthless honesty with myself about my own fears. As I worked on each of the twelve steps of living without fear, I tried to take each step for myself. This fifth step turned out to be one I particularly needed to retake.

Late one night last summer, I sat alone in my study. My desk was piled high with notes and research about the fear caused by our estrangement from ourselves. I began to pray about how to put into words what I had learned about this important step. I had planned to write about Paul and a few contemporary people who had discovered the power of self-acceptance and approval. I had no intention of sharing my own experiences.

That should have tipped me off. I usually avoid being personal when something I'm trying to write or preach about is needed in my own life. It's so much easier, and safer, to talk about theory and illustrate it with anecdotes from other people's lives. But who wants to hear an impersonal sermon or read a safe and cautious book?

An Unusual Exercise

As I thought about this fifth step, the Lord put me through an exercise that forced me to experience it in a new and fresh way. I had always thought of myself as a person with a healthy self-acceptance—problems and all. But that night I discovered a deeper level of the Lord's love for me than I had experienced in thirty-nine years of being a Christian.

Here's how it happened. After what seemed like a long time of silence, the Lord gave me a very strange instruction. I didn't hear His voice audibly, but the words that He formed in my mind were impelling.

"Lloyd," the Lord said, "close your eyes. Now form in your mind's eye an image of yourself."

I couldn't do it! The image wouldn't form in my mind. That in itself was very revealing to me. How had I gotten so out of touch with me? It had been a busy year, with an endless succession of long, exhausting days and short nights for rest.

My friend Ralph Osborne often cautions me, "Take care of Lloyd!" Had I failed to do that? Or more precisely, had I been so engulfed in my projects and prayers for others that I had not allowed the Lord to care for me? And on an even deeper level, had I overlooked keeping in touch with the Lord about my own fears and failures?

It was probably a combination of all of these, and I began to have a less-than-good feeling about Lloyd. I got very unhappy with myself as I thought about all the things I should have done and all the times I was less than my best for the Lord.

I felt like J. B. Phillips, who, at the height of his career in speaking, translating the Scriptures, and writing books telling Christians their God was too small, exclaimed, "Whatever happened to Jack Phillips?"

Now the Lord showed me what had happened to Lloyd Ogilvie. I was overwhelmed with the realization that I needed a fresh experience expressed by the title of my television program "Let God Love You!"

As I enjoyed a fresh touch of the Lord's Spirit and felt His unqualified love for me, an image of myself began to form in my mind. I no longer had to block it because of self-judgment. And what I saw was the loved, joyous person the Lord released me to picture.

Then the Lord put me to a further test. "Lloyd, go put your arms around yourself. Actually picture your punitive self embracing your struggling self."

"Lord," I responded, "that's not easy. It's so much easier to embrace and encourage others. Knowing all You and I know about Lloyd, do You still want me to embrace him? What about that improvement program we've been working on? What about the inadequacies and insufficiencies?"

"Do it!" the Lord commanded.

I followed orders. As I dared to embrace myself in an extension of the Lord's gracious embrace, I felt a deeper self-acceptance than ever before. A profound inner peace flooded me, followed by a new resiliency and freedom. With tears streaming down my face, I sat there praising the Lord that in spite of everything, I could be a priest to myself. I could offer Christ's love, forgiveness, and acceptance to the needy person inside.

Now, I'm not suggesting that we become involved in some kind of spiritualized narcissism, an unhealthy preoccupation with self, nor am I recommending sloppy subjectivism. Rather, the final link in experiencing Christ-centered, Cross-oriented healing grace is to fully embrace ourselves. Reconciliation with ourselves will give us freedom to love, not fear ourselves. The result will be a greater willingness to allow the Lord to continue to change the very things that frighten us about ourselves. And as those changes occur, we'll be amazed at our new ability to embrace others.

All this has an authentic basis in Scripture. Let's turn our attention to one of the most personal, autobiographical passages in Paul's epistles.

How Paul Embraced Himself

In 1 Corinthians 15, Paul allows us to get inside his mind as he embraces himself as a man in Christ. "By the grace of

God I am what I am, and His grace toward me was not in vain; but I labored more abundantly than they all, yet not I, but the grace of God which was with me" (v. 10).

That personal parenthesis comes in the midst of Paul's soaring rhetoric about Christ's death for our forgiveness, His resurrection for our victory over death, His appearances to Peter, James, the other apostles, and last of all, to Paul himself. The appearance of the risen Christ was very important to Paul because it was his badge of apostleship.

But not everyone in the early church accepted that. Some questioned his authority. Others differed sharply with his policy of accepting Gentile converts into the church. Paul seems to have this criticism in mind as he speaks here of his encounter with Christ on the Damascus Road.

"Then last of all, He was seen by me also, as by one born out of due time. For I am the least of the apostles, who am not worthy to be called an apostle, because I persecuted the church of God" (1 Cor. 15:8–9). Paul then goes on to declare his grace-rooted self-acceptance, "But by the grace of God I am what I am. . . ."

I am convinced that this healthy, fearless self-acceptance in the context of the Lord's love for him explains why Paul was one of the most loving, forgiving, adventuresome, courageous human beings who ever lived. In this passage giving the progression of the apostle's experience, we discover the three elements of a Christ-motivated self-embrace.

What We Were Apart from Grace

First, Paul shows us that embracing ourselves begins with an honest recognition of what we were apart from God's grace. He talks frankly about that. The Apostle honestly admits that his early self-hate had been transferred to angry persecution of the church. In describing what he was before meeting Christ, Paul purposely used a condemnatory phrase his enemies were using against him, "one born out of due time."

There have been many different interpretations of what Paul meant by this. Some suggest that he meant that if he had been born earlier, or in Galilee rather than in Tarsus, he would have responded to Jesus' ministry and become one of His disciples. But actually, Saul of Tarsus was probably a student of Gamaliel in Jerusalem at the time of Jesus' ministry, death, and resurrection. And for him to have been appointed to purge the early church, he must have been a Pharisee in high authority in the Jewish leadership in Jerusalem.

I think Saul had known about Jesus of Nazareth. He had watched the events of His death from an angry, judgmental distance and scoffed at the rumors of His resurrection. When Christ's apostles claimed He was alive, Saul gladly accepted the bloody task of attacking the church, for now he had a cause to match his turbulent, hostile heart.

But I think the best way to interpret Paul's identification of himself as "one born out of due time" is to stick to the literal meaning of the Greek word he used. It means "miscarriage" or "untimely birth." That Greek word is what some called him, and Paul simply accepted it. His new birth in Christ had not happened the same way as the other apostles'. Not only was it later, it was unexpected and unwanted by some. Rather than being defensive, Paul could say, "Christ appeared even to me, a miscarriage." He knew that at the time Christ chose and called him, he was a kind of miscarriage in that he was destroying his birthright as a child of God. But whatever others had said about Paul was nothing in comparison to what he said about the kind of person he was before he received the Lord's grace.

But through Christ's regenerating process Paul had become a new person. During his fourteen years of prayer and preparation after his conversion and before his first missionary journey, the Lord worked within his mind and heart to produce a miracle. Paul wrote about this transformation in his second letter to the Corinthian Christians: "Therefore, if anyone is in Christ, he is a new creation; old things have passed away; behold, all things have become new. Now all things are of God, who has reconciled us to Himself through Jesus Christ, and has given us the ministry of reconciliation . . . " (5:17–18). That transformation was the second reason Paul was able to put his arms around himself.

Humble Praise

Knowing that "all things are of God," Paul could give humble praise for the person he had become and all that had been accomplished through him. That praise made it possible for him to say, "By the grace of God I am what I am, and His grace toward me was not in vain" (1 Cor. 15:10). The grace of God in Christ had reached the depths of Paul's prior self-negation and healed him to the extent that he could take delight in the new person he'd become.

One thing is sure—we know that we have experienced the full transforming power of God's love when we can say, "By His grace, I am what I am. It hasn't been in vain." The Greek word Paul used for "vain" means "empty." God's grace was full and overflowing. And as part of the overflow, Paul couldn't stop praising the Lord for all He had done. To have refused to embrace the new grace miracle of himself would have been blasphemy.

We Are Not Self-Made People

Let's face it. Most of us are not self-made women and men. We are what we are by God's grace alone. Knowing that does not engender pride but praise. It spurs us on, anxious to discover more grace.

Near the end of his life Paul had that fine blend of fulfilled unfulfilledness. "Not that I have already attained, or am already perfected; but I press on, that I may lay hold of that for which Christ Jesus has also laid hold of me" (Phil. 3:12).

That's it! The more we embrace what the Lord has accomplished in us, the more we want to press on. Embracing ourselves frees us also to reach out and "hug" the future.

Paul wrote the Colossians, "Let no one cheat you of your reward, taking delight in false humility" (2:18). Good advice! Let's not cheat ourselves with a false humility that magnifies our weaknesses. All this does is to make us so down on ourselves that we can't praise God for the miracle He's pulling off in our character and personality.

This truth is beautifully illustrated by the story of the scholar Mauretis, who was picked up along the side of the road, ill with malnutrition, and brought into a hospital. Two doctors consulted about what they should do with him, and both decided just to let him die because he was a "worthless human being." Hearing what they said, he gathered the last bit of his strength, sat up in bed, and said, "Physicians, listen! Can you call anyone worthless for whom Christ died?"

A good question. What right do we have to call ourselves worthless? Or inadequate? Or insufficient? Or a failure? Christ died for us and lives in us!

As I look back over my life, God has been so good. The only word I can use to describe His goodness is that it includes many "serendipities"—unexpected surprises. God has intervened to give me strength when I was weak, insight and wisdom when I had little of my own, and power when I could not generate it myself.

R. C. Sproul exemplifies this. Today, he is an outstanding Christian writer. And yet, when he was in the eighth grade, his classmates said, "Sproul, you can't write!" His teacher knew better. One of his papers was so remarkable that the teacher put it up on the board and said, "Don't let anyone ever say that R. C. Sproul can't write!"

Now, years later, Sproul is writing about the depths of the mysteries of God. When he received a manuscript back from his publisher, he read just the first page. It was full of the editor's corrections. All the feelings from eighth grade came flooding back, and he said, "If the rest of the pages are like that"—and he multiplied the number of pages by the number of corrections on the first page—"then there must be ten thousand corrections in that manuscript! 'R. C. Sproul can't write!'" And then he went back over it and asked for the Lord's blessing on his effort. When he had finished, he remembered the words of the teacher, "Don't let anyone ever say that R. C. Sproul can't write."[1]

Heroic Service

Paul's embrace of himself as a new creation in Christ not only enabled honest confession and humble praise, but also led him to the third step of embracing himself. He became involved in heroic service. That's always the sure test of the "I am what I am by grace" embrace of self-acceptance. Paul said, "I labored more abundantly than they all, yet not I, but the grace of God which was with me" (1 Cor. 15:10).

And it was true. None of Paul's critics, not even the other apostles, accomplished what the Lord did through Paul's missionary journeys in Asia and Europe, Jerusalem, Ephesus, Athens, Rome—the centers of human religions, commerce, philosophy, and power. All felt the impact of a transformed Pharisee who knew Christ's embrace, embraced himself, and was free to embrace others from the least to the mighty.

More Than Just a Hug

"We're here for our hugs!" a man said after a worship service recently. I had watched him and his wife approaching as I greeted the congregation leaving the church. He was at least six feet, five inches tall and wore a big cowboy hat and western boots. His wife appeared to be half his height. The brim of his hat hit me on the middle of my forehead as he stood close, waiting for my response.

As I tried to reach around the bulk of his big shoulders he said, "My lady and me watch your program every week back on our ranch in Idaho. We see you huggin' people sometimes while they run them credits on the end. So I says to the missus here, 'Let's save up and go out there and get our hugs.' So here we are!"

I gave the rancher and his wife a big hug. Later, in conversation, I realized what they really needed was an embrace that included listening to their needs as people and their desire to know Christ personally.

As the couple talked on, I prayed, "Lord, these people really need the embrace of Your grace. Give me strength to care for them. Give them the gift of faith to trust You and turn their lives over to You."

It happened. They made a commitment. They had come for a hug which I gladly gave them, but they then experienced something far greater—the loving embrace of the Lord Jesus. Now they are hugging people in Idaho and no longer need to travel 750 miles to our church to get a hug.

I've come to see that while some people who are uncomfortable with a physical hug have an almost overpowering need for the warm spiritual embrace of caring friendship. In fact, I believe that most of us respond readily to a person who is honestly interested in us. We're hungry for deep and caring relationships in which we can be wholly ourselves and talk about how to live our faith in the stresses and pressures of life.

An alcoholic who has learned that I stop at a particular doughnut shop some mornings on the way to my study positions himself by the door of the shop waiting for me to come by. He always needs money and some conversation. The other day he greeted me by saying, "I'm here for you!" What he meant was that he knew my schedule and was waiting for me.

But his words had a deeper meaning. In a real way, he was there for me. I needed to give as much as he needed to receive. And the more secure I am in the Lord's grace the freer I am to realize that reaching out to people like that man is as important as getting to my study to write a sermon on loving!

Reaching Out

I felt that recently when I had the privilege of preaching at the Women's Prison in Chino, California. Father James Fallon, a Roman Catholic priest who has become a good friend of mine, is one of the prison chaplains. Father Jim asked me to come and speak to a group of the women who watch our television program.

When I arrived, the room was crowded with inmates. Every crime imaginable had been committed by these women, but I saw them as people in desperate need of Christ's loving embrace. He was there in power as Father Jim led the meeting and I talked about the cross and how to receive grace and begin a new life.

Tears streamed down those women's faces as they responded to the Lord's love. At the end of the service, I gave a simple invitation. All but two women stood up and came forward. It took us an hour and a half to pray for all of them.

Every so often during that hour and a half I looked over at Father Jim, and his face was radiant as he nodded to me and seemed to be saying, "Go on, go on, this is the Lord's moment!"

One woman said, "I've never seen my little boy. I've been here eight years. I've got five more years. He's going to be thirteen years old before I ever see him. Pray that God will take care of him. I want to become a Christian tonight."

A tall woman with a mixture of expressions on her face asked for help to be able to give her life to the Lord and allow Him to love her. She'd committed three murders and had been in prison for fifty years. She had not been paroled in previous hearings because the first question the parole board asked her each time was, "Are you repentant of the crime you committed?" And she'd say, "What crime?" But that night she said to me, "Please pray that I can receive God's love and accept His forgiveness and be honest with the parole board." After I prayed for her, I gave her a hug and thanked her for being my new sister in Christ.

On the way home, Father Jim said to me, "No one but the Lord could have done what happened tonight." He was right. With the Lord's arms around us, we had been used to embrace those desperate women with His love and hope.

But we don't need to go to a prison to find people who are imprisoned and need our love. They are in our families, in our churches, at work, and everywhere in our communities. They need our love and encouragement.

There's a direct relationship between our daily experience of God's grace and our willingness to communicate His grace to other people. The more we accept ourselves as loved by the Lord, the more we'll be free to let go of our fear of ourselves. Pretentious pride and false humility are both unnecessary. We can say with Paul, "I am what I am by the grace of God."

God knows our failures and has forgiven us. He knows our potential and affirms us. We dare not do less for ourselves. So embrace yourself!

Step 6 _____

I will admit I am inadequate
to meet life's opportunities,
but I will conquer my fear
by becoming a riverbed for the flow
of God's guidance, love, and power.

_____

The Gift of Inadequacy

I WANT TO GIVE YOU A GIFT.

It's one I need to receive every hour of every day. It is the gift of freedom to accept the idea that all of us are inadequate.

That is probably the last gift in the world you ever expected me to want to give you. In fact, you probably expected my gift to be one of affirmation for your talents and abilities. As you know from reading this far, I believe in affirmation, but it does contain a built-in difficulty. It tends to build up a false confidence in our own strength, and God always has a way of pressing us beyond our own capabilities. So, if we only tout other people's skills, or even their untapped potentials, we mislead them into believing they will always have what it takes.

No one has what it takes. The truth is we *are* inadequate for the constantly changing, ever-escalating opportunities of life. We become gripped with fear when we try to be adequate on our own, because that simply isn't possible.

But in reality our feelings of inadequacy are a blessing.

They can lead us to the next giant step in overcoming the fear of living.

So, here's step number six for living without fear: *I admit I am inadequate to meet life's opportunities, but I will conquer my fear by becoming a riverbed for the flow of God's guidance, love, and power.*

A Turning Point

How does this life-changing step work?

A few years ago, a man came to see me to tell me about his fear of being inadequate to handle the many personal and professional problems that were confronting him.

"Up until now," Alex said, "I've been able to take life in stride. I've never felt inadequate to step up to bat and hit the ball out of the park, so to speak. But now I've been given more responsibilities at work, and at the same time, one of my sons is in real trouble. I've used all the self-affirmation and thought-conditioners I know for developing a positive attitude.

"I stand before the mirror when I shave in the morning and say, 'Alex, you can do it; you've got what it takes, so believe in yourself. You've been a skyrocketing success at work and a model father. You can win, Tiger, you can win!'

"But by the end of the day, I realize that the pep talk didn't work. I really fear messing it up at work, and my boy has me on the ropes. For the first time in my life I really feel inadequate."

"Perhaps you *are* inadequate," I said quietly, with a feeling of empathy.

Alex was stunned. He looked at me intently, disappointment and shock written all over his face. He looked like I'd just punched him in the stomach with a hard jab.

"What do you mean?" He was indignant. "I came to see you to get a lift, not have my worst fear confirmed and increased. I needed you to cheer me on, not put me down."

At the very least, I had Alex's attention.

"My friend," I said, "you are on the edge of making one of life's most crucial discoveries. You are ready for a lift-off to a new level of life. You know that you are a talented and highly trained professional. And we both know how much you love your kids. In both areas you are being pressed with challenges where you are inadequate—by yourself. You need God's help.

"He's ready to use abilities you didn't know you had and multiply your efforts with the gifts of wisdom, vision, and power only He can provide. The feeling of inadequacy can either be the source of discouragement or the beginning of new courage. You don't have all that's needed for this time in your life, but God does and He wants to help you."

At that time in his life, Alex was one of those Christians who had a vague faith. And for the first time, he was up against difficulties beyond his human resources.

We talked at length about how Christ wanted to live in him and give him supernatural power. We discussed the great things He had done through people who depended on Him. Not only were their own abilities expanded, but they were also given discernment, insight, ideas, solutions, and inventive genius beyond anything they could have produced on their own.

Then I shared with Alex the secret of how to receive that supernatural power: (1) a total surrender of our challenges; (2) an invitation for Christ to live in us; (3) an intimate, dependent relationship with Him, and (4) a willingness to give Him the glory when we perform beyond our human adequacy.

We ended our discussion with prayer. Alex confessed his inadequacy and asked the Lord to fill him with superhuman adequacy. It was then that Christ came into Alex's life with His love and power. Day by day, as he began to rely on the Lord's adequacy, Alex received the wisdom and strength he needed for his challenges at work and with his family.

That turning point in Alex's life took place several years ago. Since then, he's faced bigger and more demanding opportunities at work than he ever thought would be entrusted to him. And the challenges at home and in the rest of his life haven't stopped either. Each new challenge keeps him on the edge of new growth in Christ.

Just recently when I ran into Alex he said, "Life doesn't get easier, but it sure does get more exciting. The moment I get comfortably settled on a plateau thinking I can handle things myself again, I get pushed into some new responsibility beyond what I can tackle alone. The great thing is that the bigger the problem or the chance to try something really innovative and creative, the more strength and skill I'm given. The hardest part is remembering to let everyone around me know that the Lord gets the glory. Don't ever let me forget that!"

"I won't," I replied with a smile. "And don't let me forget it either."

We've become brothers in that pact. It's encouraging to have a friendship in which we both can admit our fear of inadequacy and remind each other that Christ is going to keep pushing us beyond our abilities so that we can be riverbeds for the flow of more of His power through us.

Keeping Life Pared Down

In recent years we've heard a lot about the "Peter Principle"—the theory that people rise in life to the level of their incompetence. Certainly, that's true for lots of people who rise to a level beyond their abilities and bungle the opportunities they are given. But here is an "Ogilvie Principle"—as Christians, we should constantly be rising to the level of our human inadequacy, for only then can we discover the amazing gift of Christ's adequacy.

Unfortunately, many Christians fall into a crippling trap.

They rise to the level of their inadequacy and are gripped with the fear of being inadequate. Instead of receiving Christ's power to make them adequate, they are filled with panic about not having what some relationship or responsibility will require.

In response to that panic, many of us keep life pared down to our human limitations. "I'd never be able to do *that!*" we exclaim. Or, "You'll never catch me attempting that. I'd fall on my face." Or, "Leave the heroics to someone else. I'll stick to what I'm sure I can do on my own."

That attitude, though, is deadly and life-paralyzing. We settle for a supine smallness of vision.

But that doesn't work for long. The moment we think we have life narrowed down to what we can handle, we are confronted with unexpected intrusions into our constricted little world.

It is true that we all have problems that make us feel inadequate. But we can be sure that when these are solved there will be others, probably bigger ones than we ever thought we would have to wrestle with. We can also be sure that the Lord will give us more to do and more to attempt for Him than we will ever be able to handle alone. We can know beyond any question that God will give us the ability to meet every challenge He places before us.

In fact, I'm convinced that unless we are attempting something we could not pull off on our own strength, we have surrendered to the fear of being inadequate. As a result we become timid and shrink back from attempting what we know we are called to do. We refuse to take the next step in our spiritual growth.

My Own Experience

That fear of inadequacy haunted me through many years of my life. The longing to be adequate was a false god for me through the early years of my Christian life. It was rooted in feelings of inadequacy in my youth, which carried over into my Christian experience.

Accomplishments, degrees, and recognition did little to feed my voracious hunger to be recognized as an adequate person. The therapy that was a part of my training to be a pastoral counselor helped me see that the causes for my feelings were contained in certain family and adolescent experiences. But that self-understanding did little to offset the feeling that some day people would discover how inadequate I really was. I tried to hide my fear behind a highly polished exterior of adequacy. But that became a barrier to deep relationships with people and kept me from discovering the secret of freedom in Christ.

This scenario occurred early in my ministry, because I was given opportunities that exceeded my human capabilities, and I knew I could not make it on my own. Finally, when I confronted this honestly, the Lord gave me a three-part gift to be able to admit my inadequacy and receive His power.

1. A Lesson from My Heroes

The first part of the gift opened my eyes to a most important truth that had eluded me. Everywhere I turned in my Bible study and in my reading of the biographies of great Christian leaders, I was struck by a common theme. Their encounter with Christ spurred them on to attempt the impossible. The Lord constantly pressed them beyond their human capabilities. It was in the dangerous interface between what they were and what He called them to be that they discovered His power. And in drawing on that power they persistently took risks with raw faith. The greater the risk, the more faith and daring they received.

It was then that I began to see that by trying to be adequate I was cutting myself off not only from the flow of the

Lord's power, but from the humanly impossible things He wanted to do through me.

2. No Time to Relax

The second part of the Lord's gift was to help me realize that I will never be able to rest easy at any level of growth. It became obvious that one accomplishment was always followed by some new challenge or some problem way beyond my abilities to face or solve. There was never time to sit back and savor success. Ever present were new and fresh challenges that kept me aware of my inability to cope without the Lord's intervention and strength. It was a great relief to accept, finally, that this is the way it's always going to be. Right up to the last day of my physical life!

3. The Fellowship of the Inadequate

The third part of the gift came in what I call the "fellowship of the inadequate." The Lord gave me a group of people with whom I met each week. We studied the Bible, shared our needs, and prayed for each other. Every person in the group was highly successful in some area, and yet all felt this same sense of being inadequate for the challenges entrusted to them. The Lord had arranged for people with a common need to be my fellow-adventurers.

The group was galvanized into oneness. The Lord was consistently giving us awesome challenges that forced us to realize that we were inadequate without Him and that we needed each other's support and prayers. Each time one of us would be close to victory over some soul-sized problem, someone would say, "Now that the Lord's won that battle, get ready for the next one!" And sure enough, usually in the next week or two some opportunity would develop to convince us of our inadequacy and His amazing adequacy for our needs. This was a great learning and growing experience for me because I learned never to trust myself to attempt the adventure in Christ alone.

Timothy and the Spirit of Fear

We have a colorful example in the New Testament of how the Apostle Paul helped Timothy to overcome feelings of inadequacy so he could move on to accomplish what the Lord had called him to do. In fact, what we know as the second letter to Timothy was sent to encourage and inspire the youth to rise above his feelings.

Young Timothy as you will remember was converted to Christ when Paul visited his home town of Lystra on the first missionary journey. Then when Paul was in Lystra on his second missionary journey, he enlisted Timothy to be a fellow worker with him as he moved around Galatia, Macedonia, Greece, and the province of Asia. And eventually Timothy was left in charge of the church at Ephesus.

This was not an easy assignment because Ephesus was a "vanity fair" of pagan worship, secularism, and hostility to Christ and His followers. Trying to guide this group of new Christians was a severe test for Timothy as he faced difficulties that far exceeded his human abilities.

It is possible Timothy had a lifelong struggle with feelings of inadequacy. It is also possible these feelings were nurtured by the fact that he was naturally timid and was not physically strong. At any rate, it is apparent that the Ephesian challenge had Timothy "on the ropes" and Paul spoke to his need for courage in the second letter to his young friend. What we have here is kind of a last will and testament of Christian courage. A close look at Paul's advice for Timothy will be helpful to us.

No Easy Reassurances

Paul didn't try to cheer Timothy on with easy reassurances of the young disciple's human talents and strengths.

Instead, the Apostle reminded him of what the Lord had done in his life and what He would continue to do that would more than meet his feelings of inadequacy.

But there was something Paul wanted Timothy to do in preparation to receive what the Lord wanted to give him: "Therefore I remind you to stir up the gift of God which is in you through the laying on of my hands" (2 Tim. 1:6). What was this gift Timothy had received that Paul wanted him to stir up? It was the greatest gift of all—the indwelling Spirit of the living Christ. This is the same gift Paul encouraged the Galatian Christians to claim, "And because you are sons, God has sent forth the Spirit of His Son into your hearts . . . " (Gal. 4:6).

The Spirit of Christ had set a fire of vision and conviction burning in Timothy. Fellowship with Paul, Silas, and Luke had kept that flame ablaze as they had traveled together and encouraged each other in the ministry of evangelism. Now, alone in leadership in Ephesus, Timothy needed to rekindle Christ's fire within him. Paul didn't tell him to try harder or pray longer. Instead Paul told him to get back to the source of his supernatural strength.

Stirring up the Fire

Paul's advice to Timothy applies to us because we have a part in being on-fire Christians. We can allow the fire of Christ's Spirit to be smothered with neglect or resistance. But by far the greatest cause of our fire's fizzling out is the effort to be faithful disciples on our own strength. We try to run on our own resources and are not fueled by constant dependence on the Lord. Sometimes we even try to live the Christian life without Christ!

The only cure is to stir up the banked fires within us. Clarence Jordan translates Paul's admonition in a vivid way, "I'm reminding you to shake the ashes off the God-given fire that's in you." In other words, shake the grate until the embers are exposed, use the poker to push the coals together, and then use the bellows to blow them into flaming life. That's exactly what we do when we face a challenge or responsibility beyond us and cry out for Christ to refuel the fire within us with a fresh infilling of His Spirit.

God Is Not the Source of Fear

Paul next reminds Timothy that God is not the source of fear of any kind, including the fear that comes from feelings of timidity or inadequacy: "God has not given us a spirit of fear" (2 Tim. 1:7). The particular Greek word for fear used here is *deilia*, a word always used in a bad sense for "cowardice" or "timidity." And why do we so often have feelings like those? Because we don't think we have what it will take to confront and handle life's soul-stretching problems—we feel inadequate to cope.

The word "spirit" as it's used in verse 7 means "a pervading mood, attitude, and mode of thinking." In other words, the spirit of fear cripples us with caution and reserve. It limits what we are willing to attempt to only those things we are sure we can do on our own strength. We get all wrapped up in ourselves—usually a very small package!

The spirit of fear manifests itself in a panic over criticism and an unhealthy concern over what others think. Fearing failure, we attempt very little. The spirit of fear can also spread to groups and even pervade a church congregation. When leaders are more concerned about being adequate than being on fire with Christ, their timidity and cowardice water down the robust preaching of the Gospel. As a result, the dynamic impact of the church on society is lost.

Paul makes it clear to his young friend that the kind of fear he's talking about does not come from God. It is brought on by feelings of inadequacy that straight-jacket the creativity and freedom of God's Spirit. And, unfortunately, the deadly fear of inadequacy locks us into a level of inadequacy. On the other hand, if we turn that fear over to the Lord and let Him heal it, we are released to attempt the great things He wants us to do.

Paul then follows up by saying that the indwelling Spirit of Christ offers us "power, love and a sound mind" (v. 7). Since Paul often puts the key word last after the conjunction "and," I'd like to review the Spirit's supernatural adequacy in us by considering these gifts in the order that they are usually given in our experience. A sound mind precedes the ability to love, and the commitment to love leads us to ask for spiritual power.

The Spirit of a Sound Mind

The first gift of the Spirit's activity in us to make us adequate is a "sound mind." The Greek word Paul uses here is descriptive of a Spirit-anointed, disciplined mind, one totally under the control of the Spirit of Christ. It is a mind able to think His thoughts, and see the potential of people and situations the way He does. In a sound mind the powers of imagination are whole and healthy. With a sound mind the Christian focuses on the Lord's vision for the specific opportunities of life.

Or, to put it another way, a "sound mind" overcomes fears of inadequacy by a Spirit-produced thinking or attitude about those things we are to do and the resources we need and will be given to accomplish them. A Christ-inspired, "sound mind" provides reliable guidance and a clear vision. It lifts our focus beyond what we can do in our own strength to what the Lord wants to do through us.

Let's face it. We need the Lord's help in every relationship, situation, and problem where life dishes out challenges beyond us. Wherever we feel inadequate—in marriage, with our families, on the job, in our opportunities to share our faith, and in the impossible tasks the Lord has given us to do—we need to confess, "Lord, I can't make it on my own; this is beyond me; I just don't have what it takes!"

To such a prayer, I believe His response would be, "Good—you were never meant to be adequate on your own. Now, relax and allow Me to think through your mind and I'll reveal *My* strategy and show you how you will accomplish it with *My* strength." We don't have to thrash about with uncertainty. The Lord will guide and provide.

The Spirit of Love

A sound mind is able to conceive and transmit to our emotions the assurance that we are loved by the Lord. We not only know we are loved by the Lord, but we *feel* loved. His Spirit of love flows into and through us. Most of the challenges of life that make us feel inadequate are those in which we are called to love beyond our human ability. Think of the people you find it difficult to love as much as they need to be loved. Reflect on the people who have hurt you whom you find it impossible to forgive. Focus on the people who demand more of your time and resources than you feel capable of giving. Or consider the situations in which you need to give yourself sacrificially and want to pull back. Again we protest, "Too much, Lord, the needs of people are greater than I can meet!"

And yet, the great need in the world is for Christians with passion. Passion is Christ's intense love burning in us for people and human suffering. John Henry Jowett, a great preacher of a past generation, wrote, "The gospel of the broken heart demands the ministry of bleeding hearts . . . as soon as we cease to bleed, we cease to bless . . . we can never heal the needs we do not feel. Tearless hearts can never be the heralds of Christ's passion."

A passion for the needs of people, a broken and bleeding heart really makes us feel inadequate. To see the suffering and realize what love demands, creates the most desperate sense of insufficiency. That's why a sound mind capable of thinking with the Savior and feeling with His heart the need for love for the people around us, leads us to accept the third of the gifts Paul listed for Timothy in his antidote to the fear of inadequacy.

The Spirit of Power

Paul then tells Timothy that the Christian is not only to have the Spirit of a sound mind and the Spirit of love, but also the Spirit of power. The Greek word he uses here for power is the root from which our word "dynamite" comes—an enabling and dynamic power. We can be assured that the Lord never calls us to do anything for which He is not willing to provide the power. In other words, it isn't that "We are able!" but "The Lord is able!"

Paul underlined this point clearly to the Ephesian Christians: "Now to Him who is able to do exceedingly abundant above all that we ask or think, according to the power that works in us, to Him be glory in the church by Christ Jesus to all generations, forever and ever. Amen" (3:20–21).

The key phrase for us here is "according to the power that works in us." As we experience that "power" and learn to depend on it, we will be free of the feeling of inadequacy.

But there's more. Receiving the power of the Spirit not only multiplies the effectiveness of our human faculties, but it also gives us supernatural abilities. We are given "understanding" *beyond* our intellectual capabilities, "love" *beyond* our natural love, "strength" *beyond* our energies. It's what Christ does through us, not what we are able to do for Him, that accomplishes lasting results.

The Healing of Randy

I had a personal experience that illustrates the message of this chapter. It happened through a miracle of healing that took place in a young man named Randy.

At the conclusion of a Sunday morning worship service

that focused on the theme of Christ's healing power, I invited people to come forward for prayer with the pastors and elders for healing of the spiritual, emotional, physical, and circumstantial needs of their lives. I was astonished by the response. Several hundred people filed forward and knelt across the front of the sanctuary and up the aisles.

As I looked out on the crowd of kneeling people, I was overcome by a wave of the feeling of inadequacy. "How can I meet all these needs?" I cried out to the Lord from my heart. "You can't," He seemed to say, through my thoughts. "You were never meant to and you should not try. Simply claim My healing power for each person and pray for them in My Name. Leave the results to Me!"

Along with the other pastors and elders, I moved from person to person listening to their requests for help. Then I simply prayed in the name of Jesus for healing for the needs expressed—the hurting bodies, broken hearts, and distressed relationships.

Off to the side of the chancel, by the west wall of the sanctuary, was a man I later learned was Randy. I felt irresistibly drawn to him and laid my hands on his head as I prayed for him. There were no theatrics or human manipulations. Just a plea from Randy for the Lord's touch of healing and a prayer from the depth of my heart for His healing power to be released.

A few months later, a letter arrived from the young woman who had brought Randy to that service. This is a remarkable letter, and I share it with you to give glory to the Lord for what He did for Randy.

"Last fall I brought a dear friend of mine to church with me. Randy had stage four cancer at the time and was given less than six months to live. After the service you asked people wanting to be healed to come forward. I grabbed Randy's hand and we walked down from the balcony to the front of the church and kneeled and prayed. I knew the only thing that could save Randy at that point was the grace and love of the Lord and prayed that He would be so generous as to work through you or one of the other pastors to cast this horrible disease from Randy's body. You noticed, came close, laid your hands on him, and prayed. Randy's last scan as of a month ago showed absolutely no sign of any tumors. He is healed, 100 percent healed. Praise the Lord!!"

The Lord Did It!

The Lord did that miracle of healing. All I felt was deep passion, profound inadequacy, *and* complete trust in Christ's power. When we face the great opportunities the Lord arranges, it's not the feeling of inadequacy that's wrong but the fear of being inadequate that's rooted in a desire to be sufficient on our own. And since the challenges keep getting bigger, the luxury of always being adequate is not for us to enjoy. What we can enjoy is the assurance that the Lord will release His power in spectacular ways that are best for everybody concerned.

Humanly Inadequate, Divinely Empowered

After reading that moving letter about Randy's healing, I was especially thankful that a few years ago the Elders of our church were given the Spirit of a sound mind to see our church as a healing community. They had a passionate love for people, and a willingness to claim the Lord's power to work in, through, and around us with healing power. In addition, they overcame feelings of timidity and cowardice—fear—that could have kept us from moving ahead. Instead, they admitted their feelings of inadequacy and were open to the Lord's strategy for a healing ministry. Exciting things have been happening ever since.

But we have a continual battle with the spirit of fear in every area of our church's life. It shows up in a devotion to the past, in an inordinate love for our traditions, and in programs tailored to fit our human resources. The spirit of fear, masquerading as a sense of inadequacy, can invade our minds when we least expect it. It tries to hold us back when we consider a bold increase in mission giving, grapple with the challenge of involving all our members in personal evangelism, evaluate some expansion of program, or call our people to be accountable disciples in social needs in our community. We've spent a lot of time discussing the potentially debilitating effect of the spirit of fear in the life of the church and praying to be given a sound mind, love, and power. What a difference that makes in a church! And it will radically revolutionize our personal lives as well!

My prayer is that you will accept the gift offered at the opening of this chapter—the gift of accepting that you are inadequate, especially in the light of the Lord's mysterious way of trusting us with ever-increasing challenges.

But there's a liberating alternative to the *fear of inadequacy*. Simply admit that you are inadequate, confess the spirit of fear, and allow the Lord to be your adequacy as He fills your mind with His guidance, your heart with His love, and your life with His power!

Step 7 _____

Secure in God's love,
I will not surrender my self-worth
to the opinions and judgments of others.
When I am rejected, I will not retaliate;
when I am hurt, I will allow God to heal me.
And knowing the pain of rejection,
I will seek to love those who suffer from its anguish.

_____

The Quicksands
of Rejection

IT HURTS. WE TRY TO PRETEND IT DOESN'T MATTER, BUT it does. When we say, "I couldn't care less," we really mean, "I wish I didn't care so much!" No matter how we try to explain it away or depreciate the source, being rejected by people causes excruciating pain.

And rejection does something else. It causes fear. Memories of rejections in the past make us leery, cautious, and restrained. We flinch with fear of what people can do or say to hurt us. The last thing we want is to get close to anyone. Why should we put ourselves in a vulnerable position and risk being hurt again?

We hear a lot about phobias these days. Here's one to add to the list: "*apodokimo*phobia," the dread of rejection. And that's one phobia from which we all suffer at times. Some of us, all of the time.

The fear of rejection not only keeps us from deep relationships, it often robs us of courage. We become solicitous and compliant. Eventually like a chameleon we try to blend into the background of other people's values and attitudes.

Let's face it. We all need approval and acceptance. Often we are willing to do almost anything to keep a steady flow of both coming our way. We hedge our convictions and adjust our values in order not to do or say anything that will cause people to reject us. The result is that we need people far too much. The passion to be liked ends in panic over the possibility of being rejected.

The Many Faces of Rejection

Rejection starts early in life. Nearly all of us have painful memories of rejection in our growing years. Few escaped.

For some it might have begun with an aching suspicion that their parents favored one sibling over another. Others, who didn't battle sibling rivalry, still did not experience the esteem-building affirmation of their parents.

Many felt rejection when they did not excel in athletics. There was intense anxiety when they lined up for the choosing of teams for a ball game. It was painful to be the last one chosen or not to be chosen at all. Or think of the times we were not accepted by the "in" group of kids in the neighborhood or at school. I can remember my first infatuation and the pain of discovering that my "heartthrob" didn't even know I existed.

Who can forget the longing to be popular? Think of the times we stood with wallflower anticipation at a school dance or wondered if we would have a date for the prom.

Added to all this was the fear of failure in school and the sense of rejection when we didn't quite measure up. Pressure from parents or competition from our peers made us equate grades with our value as persons. A poor grade was like a rejection slip from life.

More Than Kids' Stuff

Only kids' stuff? Hardly. Few people were accepted by the college or university of their first or even second choice.

Some of us can still remember the anguish of opening rejection letters and questioning our worth and future hopes. Others who never made it to college or didn't finish often carry a self-imposed stigma. Those of us who did make it through to graduation found the college years filled with the same pressure to be accepted and the continuing fear of rejection that we experienced as adolescents.

As adults, we continue to face rejection; the only difference is that the stakes get higher. Now acceptance is essential to our success on the job. The hidden scars of growing up make many uneasy. Being by-passed for a long-anticipated promotion or losing a position only adds to the fear of future failure. Even the very successful tell me they worry about staying on top.

Then, too, marriage offers no guarantee of acceptance and affirmation. In fact, some of the most painful experiences of rejection can happen between husbands and wives. Constant criticism, withheld affection, or lack of encouragement cause many a spouse to feel put off or put down.

Those who go through the trauma of divorce often feel unwanted and emotionally battered. As Angela, a middle-aged friend who just received her divorce papers, explained, "I feel totally rejected. I feel like an orange with all the juice squeezed out. The best years of my life are gone, and all that's left is a broken heart and shattered dreams."

Many who are single carry the inner burden of feeling rejected. Society does little to change the self-judgment. The high priority we place on marriage often makes single people question their desirability, their attractiveness, or even their sexuality.

But whether we're married or single, successful or struggling, we all experience the painful blows of rejection at one time or another. Who hasn't felt the heartache of being rejected by a loved one or friend? What they say to or about us sets us reeling; what they do to hurt us sends us to the mat. We lie low for fear of further blows to our egos.

The Need to Belong

Rejection by a group is no less painful. It stirs unhealed memories of previous times when we didn't feel included in an inner circle of friends, or when we were not accepted by some club or organization. We all long to belong. And the more important the group is to us, the more determined we become to get in and achieve solid acceptance. Our self-esteem is often based on the friends we've acquired or the prestigious groups to which we belong. When we are excluded or ignored, we feel the piercing jab of rejection.

The church is no exception. Denominations and local congregations have theological emphases and power structures. Acceptance is often reserved for those who toe the hard line. Clique words, jargon, and familiar phrases identify us as variously acceptable to the liberal, the evangelical, the charismatic, or the traditionalist. People who don't speak our language or espouse our brand of religion are excluded, even ridiculed. False pride is mingled with fictitious assurance.

Somerset Maugham put it this way in *The Moon and Sixpence:* "It is not difficult to be unconventional in the eyes of the world when your unconventionality is but the convention of your set. It affords you then an inordinate amount of self-esteem. You have the self-satisfaction of courage without the inconvenience of danger."

That accurately describes the reason for the factions in twentieth-century Christianity. It also explains why we feel rejected by religious people who think we don't meet their standards. All too often such rejection is communicated with an assumed authority of the voice of God.

But of all the rejections of life, perhaps the most difficult to bear is the rejection expressed in people's criticisms and judgments when we fail. When we most need help to face some mistake and learn from it, we feel condemnation rather than understanding and encouragement.

When we are hurt by rejection, we are tempted to slink off alone like a wounded animal to lick our wounds. The Scottish poet Robbie Burns wrote, "I lie me doon ta grieve a while, but rise to fight again." But often our method of coping is flight, not fight. We become aloof, strained, and fearful, not only with the people who have hurt us, but with others.

The Quicksands of Rejection

You may be sinking in the quicksands of rejection right now, suffocating in the quagmire with only one hand protruding out of the oozing mire of discouragement and fear. But be sure of this: the Lord can take hold of your hand and pull you out and give you sure footing on the rock of His accepting love. From that firm foundation you can take the next crucial step in living without fear.

Step number seven: *Secure in God's love, I will not surrender my self-worth to the opinions and judgments of others. When I am rejected, I will not retaliate; when I am hurt, I will allow God to heal me. And knowing the pain of rejection, I will seek to love those who suffer from its anguish.*

That may seem like a momentous step. It will mean breaking lifelong patterns and letting go of false securities. The fear of rejection is rooted in our profound need to be loved and the false idea that other people ought to love us as much as we need to be loved. But only God can meet that aching need.

Over the years, the Twenty-seventh Psalm has helped me overcome times of rejection. It has also been a powerful guide in helping others when fear of rejection was keeping them from living courageously.

A Liberating Perspective

In this psalm the writer shows us how to gain a liberating perspective, receive power, and experience peace. We discover from him how to pray when we feel the blows of rejection. The psalmist's panic over his enemies led him to a great conviction. He did not internalize the criticism or hostility of others; nor did he fuel the fires of fear with self-negation or self-blame. His first thought was of God and his need of Him.

> The Lord is my light and my salvation;
> Whom shall I fear?
> The Lord is the strength of my life;
> Of whom shall I be afraid? (Ps. 27:1).

That's exactly what we need to affirm when we feel rejected. We need the perspective that comes with the illuminating light of the Lord. In that revealing light we can see things as they really are. We can ask ourselves, "Why am I so troubled by this rebuff? Why has this person's or group's opinion of me become so important? Could it be that what they think is more important to me than what God thinks? Do I need their acceptance more than His?"

Light for the Dark Corners

When the light of the Lord reaches into the dark corners of our memories, we are able to see how the unhealed hurts of the past have made us vulnerable to current rejections. We realize that without God's help, we will continue to be victimized by people's attitudes and reactions to us.

The painful experience of rejection actually becomes a blessing when it forces us to see that the fear of rejection has more power over us than God's power at work in us. That realization leads us to confession of the false god we've made of people's approval and to a humble prayer for profound inner healing.

An Honest Inventory

When we've reached this point we are ready, with the Lord's help, to take a close look at ourselves and what might cause others to reject us. Assured of the Lord's love, we can see ourselves as we are, asking ourselves, "Is there any truth in what people have said? Are there any eccentricities in me that would cause people to react to me the way they have? Was the criticism justified? Do I set myself up for rejection by insisting on doing or saying things that cause it?"

An honest inventory of this kind is liberating. It frees us to take responsibility for our actions. It also helps us see that in many instances we were not to blame and that the rejection was unfair and unjustified. What are we to do in such a case?

New Eyes to See People

When we think someone has been unjustly critical of us, we can let the illuminating light of the Lord help us to see with new eyes the people who have hurt us. Then we can ask with empathy, "What needs in this person caused him or her to reject me in this way? What insecurity, combative competitiveness, envy, or experience of rejection by others lurks behind what has been said or done to me?"

Rejection of others always says more about the one doing the rejecting than about those who are rejected. Lack of love, sensitivity, and caring is what causes a person to give up on others. Rejection is a final effort to play God.

The Real Enemy

But in the light of God we can also see the real power at work behind people's hostile words and actions. Satan is always ready to attack those who are trying to put God first in their lives. He uses people's rejections to influence us to question our self-worth and our status as God's chosen, called, and cherished people. Experiences of rejection eventually put us in a spiritual battle with the forces of evil that are seeking to immobilize us in fear. But the Lord is infinitely greater than Satan's crafty, demeaning designs on us.

Deliverance!

Now, the good thing about knowing the real enemy is that we can cry out for the Lord's protection and victory. We can say the courage-engendering, fear-dispelling words, "The Lord is my light *and my salvation."* For the psalmist, salvation meant deliverance from his problems and enemies. It means that for us, too, but so much more.

For us, the word "salvation" is drenched with New Testament grace and power. Immanuel, God with us, Christ the Lord is our salvation. In Christ's life, His message, death, resurrection, and present power, we discover how to overcome the fear of rejection. He is able to help us because He Himself endured the full force of rejection and overcame it.

Isaiah's prophecy of the Messiah's rejection came true in Christ's life. "He is despised and rejected by men, a Man of sorrows and acquainted with grief" (Isa. 53:3). Christ was rejected by the leaders of Israel, misunderstood by His family, and denied and betrayed by His disciples. Yet throughout His life He revealed Love incarnate.

With divine authority He declared a new way to deal with rejection. "You have heard that it was said, 'You shall love your neighbor and hate your enemy.' But I say to you, love your enemies, bless those who curse you, do good to those who hate you, and pray for those who spitefully use you and persecute you" (Matt. 5:43–44). The words have an awesome ring in the light of our discussion of rejection. Who can live that quality of love? No one! Except by Christ's power . . . .

The Secret of Loving Our Enemies

Later in His ministry, Christ revealed the secret of His power to love His enemies. Anticipating His victory over evil and death on the cross, He said, "In the world you will have tribulation, but be of good cheer, I have overcome the world" (John 16:33). And indeed He did! He rose from the dead and lives as our ever-present Lord to make us overcomers when we are hit with blows of rejection.

When we invite Him to live in us, He gives us the power to love our enemies. It is impossible to do it without Him. The sure sign that we have experienced His salvation is that we can love, bless, do good to, and pray for the very people who reject us.

And so we can affirm with the psalmist, but with Christ's Galilean accent, "The Lord is the strength of my life; / Of whom shall I be afraid?" The word "strength" can also be translated "stronghold," a place to take our stand in battle. In times of battling the fear of rejection we need both a stronghold and strength. We don't have to retreat any further. The Lord wants to heal our panic. Our realization of our need is only a reflection of the Lord's greater desire to help us.

The psalmist's troubles reminded him of his loneliness for God.

> One thing I have desired of the Lord,
> That will I seek:
> That I may dwell in the house of the Lord
> All the days of my life,
> To behold the beauty of the Lord,
> And to inquire in His temple.
> For in the time of trouble
> He shall hide me in His pavilion;
> In the secret place of His tabernacle
> He shall hide me;
> He shall set me high upon a rock (Ps. 27:4–5).

The psalmist was not talking about a physical refuge. The shelter he describes is not an edifice but a relationship. He didn't want a cloistered life away from reality, but he knew that an intimate communion with God would bring inner tranquility. He longed to be in the presence of the Lord.

Experience had taught the psalmist that God alone could steady his nerves and cool his overheated panic.

The Lord's Invitation

Our desire to turn to the Lord when we are troubled is our response to His prior invitation, "Seek My face." With the psalmist we cry out to God,

> Hear, O Lord, when I cry with my voice!
> Have mercy also upon me, and answer me.
> When You said, "Seek My face,"
> My heart said to You, "Your face, Lord, I will
>   seek" (Ps. 27:7–8).

In Hebrew, the same word means both "face" and "presence."

The Lord promised Moses that His face, His presence, would go with him and the people of Israel (Exod. 33:14). Moses' response was that he would never consider pressing on without the Lord. "If Your presence [face] does not go with us, do not bring us up from here" (Exod. 33:15). In other words, Moses said, "It's unthinkable to attempt anything without the assurance that You are with us!"

In times of rejection the Lord says, "Seek My face, come to Me with your brokenness." His anticipatory grace, beforehand love, is the inspiration of our longing to experience His healing of our hurts. God uses the times when people disappoint us; even before we cry out for His help, He is waiting to love us.

God's promise to Israel through Isaiah gives us assurance that He is more ready to help us than we may have been ready to ask. "It shall come to pass / That before they call, I will answer; / And while they are still speaking, I will hear" (Isa. 65:24). Our desire to talk with the Lord comes from Him. He gives us the courage to ask for what He is ready to give. He knows exactly what we need, and our greatest need, beneath all our surface needs, is to know that

He will never reject us. That alone can rebuild our confidence and courage.

When the Lord says, "Seek My face," we can be sure that He is ready to heal our wounds of rejection. In Christ we behold God's face. "For it is the God who commanded light to shine out of darkness, who has shone in our hearts to give the light of the knowledge of the glory of God in the face of Jesus Christ" (2 Cor. 4:6). He reminds us of His love for us on the Cross.

Tenderly, the ever-present Savior says to us, "You are hurting and I understand. But do not put your trust in people's attitudes and opinions. Trust only in Me. I know all there is to know about your strengths and weaknesses, and I will never give up on you. I will comfort you."

The King Knows

Amy Carmichael, missionary to India a couple of generations ago, told the story of how Earl Jellicoe, a British naval officer, was comforted by a letter from King George. "In the midst of a sea battle when Earl Jellicoe was being misunderstood by the nation he served faithfully, a letter came from King George, whose keen sea sense had penetrated the mist which had bemused the general public. His letter heartened the fleet. What did anything matter now? 'Their king knew.'"

"Sometimes," Amy Carmichael commented, "circumstances are so that we must be misunderstood, we cannot defend ourselves, we lie open to blame, and yet we may know ourselves clear before God and man in that particular matter."[1]

The King of our lives knows! If we are to blame, it cannot be hidden from Him. And when we are unjustly criticized or condemned, He understands. In either case, He wants to join with us in a majority opinion of two that no matter what has happened, we have a bright future and can press on without dreading the next rejection.

The Healing Power

But that's not all. Christ is the healing power of the world. And just as He heals our bodies, He can miraculously heal our broken hearts. When we surrender our hurts to Him, He mysteriously works within our thoughts and feelings to set us free.

Therefore when rejections come, our first response should be to confess that we can't take them alone. So often in those times Elisha A. Hoffman's hymn goes through my mind,

> I must tell Jesus all of my trials
> I cannot bear these burdens alone
> In my distress He kindly will help me,
> He ever loves and cares for His own.[2]

Sometimes the healing comes quickly. More often it takes place over a period of time. Like a compound fracture or a concussion, a broken heart takes time to heal.

In the healing process we begin to refocus our self-image and to see ourselves as people loved and accepted by the Lord. That realization gives us the courage to embrace ourselves. If we have made mistakes that caused people to reject us, the Lord forgives us and gives us the power to forgive ourselves.

At the same time, if the hurt has been caused by distorted attitudes in those who have rejected us, Christ gives us the strength to forgive them. He then reminds us of all the people we've hurt by rejection. That usually makes us much more ready to understand and let go of our anger.

Pleasing the Wrong Person

At this point in the healing process the Lord reminds us that our oversensitivity to people's attitudes may be caused by trying to please the wrong people. We will not be free of the potential hurts of rejection until we make pleasing God our first priority. What God thinks of us is the only thing that's ultimately important. And He has already expressed His pleasure in us by choosing and calling us to be His disciples and intimate friends.

The good news is that God's pleasure in us does not vacillate with our performance. When we fail, His love for us is steady and sure. His forgiveness is offered before we ask. And when we are rejected because we've been faithful to Him in living out our faith, He strengthens our courage to stick by our convictions.

Discipleship Is Not a Popularity Contest

Our goal as disciples is not to win a popularity contest but to serve the Master. Obedience to Him often runs counter to the values of our culture. We will get into trouble because of what we believe. Our stand on social issues may bring criticism and hostility, and our priorities will make us targets for ridicule.

I'm convinced that the reason so few of us Christians share our faith with others is that we fear rejection. Think of the times we haven't talked about what Christ means to us because we feared being categorized as pious prudes. Or recall those times when we remained silent while a person's character was assassinated with gossip, or ideas were expressed that were contrary to our convictions. It happens almost every day.

Our reluctance to do battle for truth reminds us that we're playing our lives for the wrong audience. Of course, there's a constructive way to stand for what we believe: grappling with issues rather than expressing our views with argumentative arrogance.

The other day I overheard and observed a friend named Grant communicate his convictions in a very winsome way in a conversation with a group of men. For every negative comment that was made, he had a positive thought to add. When people were put down, he balanced the maligning criticism with affirmation. And when the problems of life today were discussed, he gave a clear witness to how Christ had given him power to face and solve his own difficulties. The group couldn't write him off because of the authentic way he shared what he believed. Interestingly enough, he's the person many of these men turn to when they face problems.

Our Lord calls us to greatness. That greatness involves strong convictions we cannot compromise and actions we must take because of our faith. When we have decided to please the right person, Christ, for the right reason in the right way, rejection may be a sign that we are making an impact. But the blows of rejections are softened by the deflecting shield of His pleasure in us.

The Sublime Sublimation

A further step of Christ's healing of the hurt of rejection is the sublimation of turning our attention to others who are suffering from the same feelings. As "wounded healers" we are equipped to care and console. Often the rejections we feel from people are caused by the problems they are going through, and Christ wants to make us less sensitive to what they do and say so we can be much more sensitive to their needs.

Ruth Harms Calkin, in her book *Tell Me Again, Lord, I Forget*, relates her own experience of learning to care about someone she thought had rejected her. In a free verse poem entitled "Sensitize Me, Lord" she writes,

> I spoke to her at the bus stop
> But she turned the other way.
> My immediate reaction:
> A rush of resentment—
> She's ignoring me

She doesn't really like me
I've always suspected it
Now I know.
Suddenly she looked toward me
Startled, but sincere:
"Forgive me—I didn't see you."
(Until then I hadn't noticed
the agony lining her face.)
A hesitant pause
A catch in her voice—
"I just came from the doctor's office
Our little boy has leukemia
It's all a terrible nightmare."
Lord, Lord
What loathsome selfishness.
A mother stricken with grief
Her heart soaked with pain
An hour of black catastrophe
And I thought only of me.
Cleanse me, Lord
Sensitize me
Until my first concern is for others
And my last concern is for me.[3]

There are people all around us who are suffering inside. We must take no one for granted, however polished his or her surface may look. Remember, those who reject us are probably aching over some rejection in their own lives. And Christ wants to give us the security in Him that frees us to minister to the needs of others rather than worrying constantly about our own.

The Final Stage of Healing

The final stage in Christ's healing comes when we praise Him for all of the times He's used people to affirm and encourage us. The psalmist found great relief in remembering God's goodness. "I would have lost heart, unless I had believed / That I would see the goodness of the Lord / In the land of the living" (Ps. 27:13). Reflection on the faithfulness of God produced the psalmist's positive expectation of seeing further evidences of His intervening grace.

In a real way, we get what we look for. If we expect rejection, we'll probably signal our fear to others. It may be this fearful attitude they reject as much as anything. We all abhor our own hypersensitivity to being rejected so much that we intensely dislike it in others.

Setting Ourselves Up for Rejection

Sometimes we actually set ourselves up for rejection. Ruth Anne, a lovely young woman in our church, has battled her fears and expectations of rejection for much of her life. She explains in her own words, "I have never been able to obtain or achieve what I've wanted from life.

"Maybe it all began when I was a child. I had a loving family and we had many good times together, but there was always the fear about my father's problems with alcohol. I loved my father so much, but his troubles filled me with doubts about myself and about life.

"As I grew up I wanted more than anything to discover God's will for my life, and I wanted to be prepared to serve Him. But even when I graduated from Seminary I did not have confidence. In some ways I expected failure and rejection.

"I was excited when I was called to a small southern congregation in our denomination to serve as activity and music director. But I was met with opposition at every turn. There were deep issues involved that didn't have anything to do with me, but I was caught in the middle and felt rejected in every way. I finally left.

"Other career opportunities and even my relationships with others did not live up to my expectations. I'm sure I began to project the attitude 'You probably won't want me anyway.' And in most cases I received what I felt and feared.

"But now I am discovering a new way of life. I've been a Christian for a long time . . . but a Christian focusing on myself and my fears. Now I am finding that total abandonment to Jesus and focusing on Him is my hope. He has begun a healing process in me. I now can see people who have hurt me as the hurting people they are. This helps me experience not only receiving God's grace and mercy but also sharing it.

"I am learning to move away from my fear and expectations of rejection as I turn to Jesus for His acceptance and approval. And now I'm amazed at the way He loves me through people I had previously expected to reject me."

Becoming an Encourager

When we look back over the years, we realize how the Lord strategically placed people in our lives who believed in us and spurred us on. We've actually seen the goodness of the Lord in these people. When we were discouraged, they believed in our potential; when we were tempted to give up on ourselves, they communicated hope.

I've come to believe that the Lord balances the scales: when we are rejected by someone, He sends someone else to encourage us. In fact, when I am downhearted I actually anticipate with expectancy the person He will use to mediate His uplifting love. I pray, "Well, Lord, who will it be this time?" I've never been disappointed.

Having had that kind of help through the years, I long to be an encourager to others. And I never lack for opportunities. People express their needs in their tone of voice, the expression on their faces, and in their body language. Life is difficult for most people. A ministry of encouragement leaves us little time to nurse our own feelings of rejection.

Recently the Board of Elders and the pastors of our church had a discussion concerning the people in our lives who had made the greatest impact on us, and we considered what we remember most about them. The majority of us talked about those who had encouraged us and through that affirmation had earned the right to share their faith with us. A large number of us had been introduced to Christ by the encourager He put in our lives. The discussion pushed us to ask ourselves, "How many of us are encouragers?"

The Lord delights in surprising us in the way He sends people to us when we need help and in the opportunities He gives us to help others. That makes life an exhilarating adventure.

Wait on the Lord

Knowing that the Lord is at work gives us the patience to wait for Him to act. The psalmist concludes this psalm with that seasoned wisdom.

> Wait on the Lord;
> Be of good courage,
> And He shall strengthen your heart;
> Wait, I say, on the Lord (Ps. 27:14).

We do not have to wait for the Lord to come to us, for He has never left us. What we are to wait for is the complete fullness of His healing. The only way that this can be speeded up is to trust Him with our hurts sooner. The Hebrew word translated "wait" actually means "trust in confident expectation."

Few things make us more aware of our need for the Lord than rejection. The only final cure for the frowning face of rejection is His smiling face of love and acceptance. And the more we wait for Him, the less we'll wait in fear of future rejection.

Step 8

Today I will turn over the control
of my life to the Lord.
I will trust His control over what
I was never meant to control.
With His guidance I will take responsibility
for what He has given me to do
for His glory and by His power.

The Fear of Losing Control

ONE DAY, WHILE MY SON ANDREW WAS RIDING WITH ME IN THE car, he noticed my bad habit of putting my left foot on the brake and my right foot on the accelerator.

"Dad," he said, "you can't put on the brakes and go forward at the same time!"

We both laughed, but it made me think about people I know who fear losing control. They have a heavy foot on the brakes of their lives all the time!

When I asked people in our national television audience to write me about their greatest fears, one woman wrote a very frank letter.

"You asked us to be honest about our fears. So instead of giving you some trite, quick answer, I really thought about it. And the more I did, the more I realized that the most frightening thing for me would be to lose control.

"Oh, I don't mean flying off the handle. More than that, it's the fear of not always being able to determine what happens to me. Over the years I've liked being boss over things—I feel very insecure when I can't manage things—

my home, my family, situations. That may be wrong, but
that's the way I am!"

I appreciated the woman's honesty. To a lesser or greater
degree, all of us have the problem of needing to be in
control.

It starts when we realize the awesome responsibility we
have for our own lives. Early in life we discover that there's
a direct cause-and-effect correlation between our choices
and what happens to us. What we do and say brings both
good and bad results. The hurt of failure makes us want to
avoid further pain. We determine we must work harder to
assure success.

That's when we slam on the brakes. Avoiding failure becomes an obsession. Our grip on life becomes tighter. The
thought of losing control makes us panic. We keep life's
challenges pared down to what we can handle without failure. Having been hurt, we control how vulnerable we will
become. Much of life is held at bay.

But the process doesn't stop there. Even if we do nothing,
we can be injured by other people's mistakes. The only way
to prevent that is to control their lives, too. By telling our
families, friends, and neighbors where to go, when, and at
what speed, we hope to ensure the safety of our own vehi-
cle. Besides, pushing people around gives us a feeling of
power and competence. It soothes our secret feelings of
failure.

Sometimes our techniques of domination are quite obvious: "Do what I want or else!" we threaten. But a pout can
be just as effective as a shout when we don't get our way.
Affirmation and affection are often withheld until people
get back on the track doing what we want.

People aren't helpless puppets, though; they fight back.
"Why do you always have to do it your way?" they ask.
"Who's in charge here?" Power struggles develop in marriage, in family life, in friendships at work, in the church,
and in the community.

The fear of losing control weakens the most important relationship of life . . . our relationship with Christ. It keeps us from experiencing the full joy and delight of the abundant life.

Christ loves us and offers us His power. All He asks is that we accept His absolute control. He expects us to surrender our wills to do His will and commit our total lives—all that we are and have—to Him. Then He promises us His wisdom for our decisions, His supernatural strength for our challenges, and His love for our relationships. That's not a bad offer!

Life's Biggest Struggle

And yet, our need to be in charge of ourselves, others, and situations often makes our relationship with Christ life's biggest power struggle. We are reluctant to relinquish our control and allow Him to run our lives. We may believe in Him and be active in the church and Christian causes, but trusting Him as Lord of everything in life can be scary. Even though we pray about our challenges and problems, all too often what we really want is strength to accomplish what we've already decided is best for ourselves and others.

Meanwhile we press on with our own priorities and plans. We remain the scriptwriter, casting director, choreographer, and producer of the drama of our own lives, in which we are the star performer.

When Life Really Begins

Over the years, I've discovered that life really begins with a total commitment to Jesus Christ. I've also discovered that this decision is the missing dynamic in most Christians today. Many began the Christian life with a belief in Christ as Savior. But the implications of accepting Him as Lord of all life were either not made clear or, if they were, not taken seriously.

I was a Christian for eight years before I actually committed my life to Christ. Up to that point, I had struggled constantly to stay in charge and get Christ to help me do what I thought was best. The joy and freedom I felt when I finally handed my life over to His control made discipleship an exhilarating adventure.

And yet, I've found that I had to renew that commitment every day. As a strong-willed person, I often forge ahead with my own plans and strategies. When I make a mess of things, I realize that I have taken charge again and need to resign the management of life to Christ all over again. As I do, the floodgate is opened to the flow of His guidance for my decisions. I find His answers for my perplexities, His solutions for my problems, and His love and patience for the people around me. Once again, He intervenes to meet my challenges in unexpected and delightful ways.

I'm thankful to have discovered the secret of commitment early in my ministry. Through the years it has made me aware of my need to surrender control. It has also helped me to identify the fear of losing control in other people. I've enjoyed helping uptight, tied-down people experience the freedom of allowing Christ to run their lives.

Some of those I've worked with have been religious people who didn't know Christ personally. Others have been active church members who had missed the key of surrender. Still others have been nonbelievers who banged into problems that brought them to the end of their ropes.

Living by Faith Is a Risk

The highly controlled person finds it difficult to trust Christ profoundly. Living by faith—the daring, adventuresome faith that can meet tough challenges—is risky. Feeling threatened we shrink back and refuse to take responsibility for what the Lord has put in our charge.

That leads us to the next vital step of living without fear. Step number eight: *Today I will turn over the control of my life to the Lord. I will trust His control over what I was never meant to control. With His guidance I will take responsibility for what He has given me to do for His glory and by His power.*

A Parable about Irresponsible Control

In the parable of the minas in Luke 19:11–27, Jesus shows us how to take this important step. He reveals that the fear of losing control leads to failure in the very things He's assigned us to accomplish with trust in Him.

A nobleman was about to go into a far country to receive a kingdom. Before he left, he called ten of his servants to him. He gave each a *mina,* the equivalent of one hundred Greek drachmas, about sixteen to twenty dollars in our money. "Do business until I return," the nobleman said, charging the servants to invest and multiply the minas.

When the nobleman of the parable returned, endowed with the kingdom and the right to reign over the realm, he demanded an accounting from the servants. Three made their reports. One had used his mina to earn ten. He was praised and handsomely rewarded. "Well done, good servant; because you were faithful in a very little, have authority over ten cities." The second had earned five minas with his investment. Though he did not receive the same commendation as the first, he was rewarded with equal measure for his productivity and placed in control over five cities.

The third servant, however, reported, "Here is your mina, which I have kept put away in a handkerchief. For I feared you are an austere man. You collect what you did not deposit and reap what you did not sow." Out of fear rooted in totally false assumptions about the nobleman, the servant had hidden away the mina and had no profit to show.

A Dramatic Twist

A dramatic twist occurs at the end of the parable. Dismayed by the servant's cautious unproductivity, the nobleman took his one mina away and gave it to the servant who had multiplied his investment to ten minas. I think the main part of the parable ends at this point. In verse twenty-five, however, there is a parenthesis which at first seems to be part of the parable. "But they said to him, 'Master, he has ten minas.'"

Further reflection leads me to suggest that it was Jesus' disciples who interrupted him because of the sudden, astounding turn in the parable when the unprofitable servant's one mina was given to the one who had ten. The disciples were following the story with keen, rapt attention and blurted out their astonishment at what had happened to the one-mina man.

We can understand the disciples' strong reaction. Jesus has our attention also. One of His most disturbing statements follows with a laser thrust. It's really a warning to those who fear losing control. "For I say to you, that to everyone who has will be given; and from him who does not have, even what he has will be taken away from him" (19:26).

The Lord has turned upside down the tables of our values. What does this mean? "To everyone who has . . . ." Has what? To answer that, we need to go back over the parable and reflect on its implications for us.

Jesus' Autobiography

Right from the beginning of the parable, we catch the autobiographical tone. Clearly, Jesus is the nobleman of the parable. After the cross and resurrection, He would ascend to heaven, receive the Kingdom from His Father, and return as reigning Lord. Remember that His Kingdom means His rule over those of us who are called to belong to Him as faithful and obedient disciples. We enter that Kingdom by the gift of faith He gives us, and we live in its full joy as we accept the responsibility He gives us.

The rest of the parable is really *our* story. Each of us is one of the servants. Which one best represents how you've used the mina entrusted to you?

Two Things the Servants Had in Common

All three servants had two things in common. All were given one mina and all were given the same opportunity to invest and multiply the mina. What does the mina represent for us?

I believe that the mina is the gift of faith. All of us receive the basic gift of faith. It is not earned or deserved. It is freely given to us to respond to the love, forgiveness, and reconciliation of the cross.

By faith we are given the power to believe and accept Christ as Lord and Savior and turn our lives over to His control. That's the beginning of the adventure of the abundant life and the assurance of eternal life.

The same gift of faith that reconciles us to the Lord also releases us to follow His orders in every area of daily life. He gives us—all of us—a new life to live for His glory. But it's in the response to that gift with power to know His will that often the similarity between Christians ends.

Two Ways the Servants Differed

Just as the three servants in Jesus' parable had two things in common, there were two radical ways they differed. There was a difference in what they did with their minas and how they were rewarded.

What does that mean for our mina, our gift of faith? The most obvious answer is that our faith is given to us to help us grow in our relationship with the Lord. Trusting His control of our lives produces growth in intimacy with Him and in the transformation of our character and personality in His image. We invest our mina as we pray in the phrases of the well-known hymn, "Have Thine own way, Lord . . . Mold me and make me after Thy will . . . Hold o'er my being absolute sway."[1]

Multiplying Our Minas

Multiplying our mina of faith means bringing all facets of our life under His control. That includes marriages, families, friendships, work, and the church. Christ is Lord of all. His Lordship extends to every realm as we surrender to Him what we do, say, and seek to be as His persons.

Now we are ready to look at the second thing the servants in Jesus' parable of the minas did not have in common. They were rewarded differently for their use of their mina. The two were rewarded to the extent that they multiplied what had been given to them. The one who hoarded his mina had it taken from him.

We Lose What We Do Not Use

What happened to the servant who refused to multiply his mina underlines a basic truth of life: We lose what we do not use.

The servant was afraid of losing control. When confronted with his failure, the servant tried to cover up his fear by questioning the nobleman's character. His accusation that the nobleman was austere, collecting what he had not deposited and reaping what he had not sown, could not have been further from the truth. The nobleman had left a deposit of a mina with each of the servants. He rightfully expected a return on his investment, rejoiced over the multiplication of the minas of the other two servants, and generously rewarded them.

The cautious servant refused to take responsibility for investing and multiplying the nobleman's mina. I think he feared doing something wrong and ended up doing nothing at all. Behind his pretentious exterior of superior prudence was a highly developed habit of control. The one-mina man was determined to run his own life. He ventured nothing and he got nothing. He lost what he had. This servant who refused to serve is the "patron sinner" of controlling people in every age.

What Does This Mean to Us?

We must ask, what does this mean to us? Clearly, the fear of failure is beneath the surface of our desire to be in control. The memory of previous failures keeps us from taking risks. We accept our mina of faith and keep it within safe, controllable boundaries. When life makes its demands and inflicts its problems, we are too scared to venture beyond what we are sure we can handle. A vague belief in Christ provides little help. As a result, we feel alone, defenseless, and filled with anxiety.

Then, like the cautious servant, many of us try to shift the blame. We complain about the Lord's management of things. We are quick to question why He has allowed us to have difficulties. The gift of faith goes unused and untested to receive the Lord's power in the very questions and difficulties we face. Like the fearful servant in the parable, we seldom use the mina of the gift of faith, and therefore it never really becomes ours.

We should not be surprised that the nobleman of the parable took the mina from the cautious servant and gave it to the servant who had ten. Why should he care? He neither claimed his mina nor used it for the purpose for which it was given to him. So, too, those of us who have been given the gift of faith to believe in Christ fail to appropriate the gift when we insist on maintaining absolute control of our lives. Opportunities to invest our faith have come and gone without our trusting the Lord for His strategy and the strength to follow orders.

That explains the application of Jesus' words, "For I say to you, that to everyone who has will be given; and from him who does not have, even what he has will be taken away from him" (Luke 19:26).

An untested, uninvested faith is no faith at all. Many of those who join the church say "yes" to carefully worded questions about their belief in Christ but then go on living self-dominated lives. When problems and challenges hit, they endure them as before, under their own control.

Should that faith be taken from them? That's really not necessary because it was never genuine faith at all. Saying the right words without accepting Christ's authority and our responsibility may be accommodated by some churches, but not by Christ. He was absolutely clear about that in the Sermon on the Mount. "Not everyone who says to Me, 'Lord, Lord,' shall enter the kingdom of heaven, but he who does the will of My Father in heaven" (Matt. 7:21). Accepting our responsibility to seek and do the Father's will requires complete trust in His Son who is with us to show us the way and provide the power to follow.

Humility

Complete trust requires something else—humility. The fear of losing control is really pride. And pride is simply the refusal to be loved and to love. True humility is the opposite. A humble person is not a mealymouthed, groveling bundle of self-effacement, but is a person who knows he or she is loved and gifted by God. Secure in that love, such an individual constantly points away from self to the source of strength. There's no room for the thought that he has all the answers for himself and others. Humility leads us to a right estimate of ourselves. And that estimate includes the realization that we are not omniscient, that we don't know everything and never will.

So just telling people who are afraid of losing control that they should stop being afraid won't work. They—we—need to face the deep inner cause: pride that's masquerading as a know-it-all sufficiency.

The fear we feel actually results from the confrontation of the Lord's Spirit with our own spirit of pride. "God resists the proud, but gives grace to the humble" (James 4:6). That resistance is registered in our souls first as fear. The Lord is invading our fortress of arrogance. Our defensive response is the fear of letting go. It is a sure sign that the Lord has singled us out for the breaking of our control over ourselves and others. The refusal to humble ourselves before Him sometimes means that He must humble us.

But the Lord never humiliates us. He has a much more effective way than that. He simply allows us to go on thinking we're running things until our control breaks down and we see how ineffective it really is. Fearing failure, we are hit by even greater failures. The people we've tried to control rebel and let us know that they are tired of being held in our grip. Then life falls apart in some situation we've been ruling with an iron hand. But at such times the Lord goes right on loving us and will help us, if we ask Him, to recover from our foolish assumptions of self-sufficiency.

The Story of Harold

Harold is a good example of this. He was a strong-willed person. Just ask his family or the people who worked with him. He was a drill sergeant, an answer man, and an authority on almost everything—all rolled into one. Behind his forced smile was a tightly held jaw of determination. He was a take-charge person.

At home things had to go Harold's way. At work his constantly repeated "It's not in the budget!" squashed the creativity of others, but there was always money for what he wanted to do.

As an officer of the Methodist church, he was known as "Mr. Methodist," and he enjoyed the recognition of his authority when the pastors would say, "Better check it out with Harold—nothing happens without his okay!"

The community organizations in his small town in the northwest were always short of volunteers for leadership and Harold was more than ready to step in.

Yes, Harold believed in Christ. And yes, he prayed for the Lord to bless his busy life. But Harold was a proud man.

Some frightening failures had hit him early in his adult life. He determined never to let that happen again. He clamped down on himself and those around him to be sure everything was kept in control. Never having had a profound experience of the Lord's love, he developed a defensive pride. Perfectionism covered his fear of failure. Humility was the last word people would have used to describe this religious man.

I met Harold at a men's retreat. His carefully controlled world had fallen apart. His daughter had rebelled in a way that exposed his failure as a father. A new pastor in his church had confronted him with the harm done by his imperious ways. On top of that, the members of his congregation had voted him out of his key position as a lay leader.

When Harold had turned to his job to build up his ego again, he found that some of his employees had reported to the president of the company how unhappy they were. Harold's control was collapsing.

It seemed as though the whole retreat on the joy of living under the control of the Lordship of Christ had been planned just for Harold. The Lord was closing in on him. And the miracle of the Lord's grace happened through the messages of the leaders of the retreat and the personal testimonies given by some of the other men. After several sleepless nights of wrestling with what he had heard,

Harold saw his fear of losing control for what it really was—pride and fear of failure.

Near the end of the retreat, Harold and I had a long conversation. He poured out what was happening to him. After sharing my own struggle with giving the Lord control of my life, I told him about several people I'd known who had overcome their tight control on life by surrendering their lives to Christ. We talked about his need to accept how much the Lord loved him and about the freedom that living under the Lord's control brings.

Then, because the Lord's Spirit was working in him, Harold was able to see his lack of humility and what his need to be in control had produced. Taking charge had kept him from his real responsibility of loving and helping the people around him. At the end of our time together, he confessed his pride, his fear of losing control, and his controlling ways in relationships. And he prayed an honest prayer of commitment to Christ.

Later in the day, Harold shared his commitment with the men in his small group, all of whom had come from his town. It was not easy to be open and honest about what he had gone through.

Some of the men in the group had experienced Harold's self-assured, controlling personality firsthand and had decided that he would probably always be that way. They were amazed at what he told them. And the same Lord who had broken open Harold's heart was there to help the men be receptive and understanding. In fact, some of them were able to confess their own need for release. The group talked about how they could help each other in the future when the old pattern of fear reared its ugly head.

I'm happy to say that group of men has continued to meet. They have breakfast together every other week to talk about how to live under the management of the Master. When they see each other around the community, they greet one another with five uplifted fingers—a finger for each of the five vital words of their group's motto, "Relax, Christ is in control!"

But Harold and his friends would be the first to tell us that the commitment they made at that retreat was only the beginning. The repatterning of their need to be in control continues daily. And the fear of losing control in some relationship or challenge is a warning signal that they have slipped back into old habits that don't work. The more they admit the tendency, the less it happens.

Six Ways to Accept Christ's Control

Each of us is different, and we all have our own ways of bucking the Lord's authority. What can we do about our fear of losing control? Here are six ways to accept Christ's control that summarize what I've tried to say in this chapter.

1.   Admit that the need to be in charge of your life has resulted in a fear of losing control. Acknowledge that this is rooted in pride and that you need to receive more of the Lord's grace in your life.

2.   Humbly tell the Lord about your panic over losing control. Accept His healing love and forgiveness for the limits you've placed on yourself and other people by always wanting to be in charge. Tell Him exactly what has happened under your insufficient management.

3.   Make today the first day of a new beginning. Commit your life to the Lord's authority.

4.   Experiment with trust and experience the results. Move quickly to the problems and needs you face right now. Take them one by one. Give them over to Christ's control.

5.   Keep a logbook in which you record what you have committed to Christ and what happens. Write a few paragraphs daily about the results of living under Christ's control. Discover how He works and note what is happening to heal your fears.

6. Ask the Lord to assign you challenges with people and situations needing His love and power. Trust Him! Through you He will do things you never thought could happen.

The Lord wants us to experience the difference. He knows that we will not give up the anxiety of being in charge until we really feel the joy of living by faith in His control.

I firmly believe that anyone who follows these six suggestions for thirty days will experience an exhilarating release and will never again be tempted to control everything and everybody again.

Take your foot off the brake!

Step 9 _____

I confess my fearful imagination
and today I ask the Lord
through His Spirit
to make my imagination a channel
of His vision
and not a breeding place of fear.

_____

It's All in Your Imagination

IT HAPPENS WHEN WE LEAST EXPECT IT.

Suddenly our peace of mind is invaded by frightening thoughts. Fearful possibilities are flashed on the screen of our minds as we picture in vivid detail the dire consequences of our actions.

Our concerns about the people we love are played out in tragic scenes. And the difficult people in our lives take leading roles as villains.

Fantasies are enacted on the stage of our minds, and we see ourselves saying and doing things that would be outrageous in real life. False pride makes us into heroes or heroines who achieve fame, wealth, and virtue in splendid scenes of pageantry.

All this takes place in the inner, hidden world of the imagination, one of the magnificent faculties of the thinking brain. Instead of using this marvelous God-given ability in a positive way, we misapply it to exaggerate our most disturbing fears.

Any serious conquest of such crippling fear in our lives

must eventually confront the tendency of the imagination to produce illusory or unreal fears and to intensify our panic over those fears that do have some foundation in reality. An imaginary fear may be unreal, but a fearful imagination is very real.

Many people who responded to my survey of the causes of fear in their lives simply wrote, "Imaginary fears." Some went on to explain that many of their worst fears never happened. And yet they continued to be victims of their gloomy imaginations.

Real-Life Examples

For example, Teresa discovered a lump in her breast. Immediately she called a specialist for an appointment, but he couldn't see her for a week and a half. Teresa says those were the longest eleven days in her life. She was paralyzed by fear as she anticipated the worst possible diagnosis.

In her imagination, Teresa actually pictured a long illness and dramatized the excruciating experience of saying goodbye to her husband and children. She kept going over and over what it would be like to die of cancer.

When she finally did see the doctor and had some exploratory surgery, the lump turned out to be benign. But until she received that report, her imagination had run wild.

Or take Lance. He's constantly worried about his job. Each year he goes through agony in the weeks just before his annual review. He pictures his boss giving him a poor report or even putting him on notice.

That has not happened in the five previous yearly reviews, but Lance still imagines the worst. In reality, he's a conscientious worker and has every right to expect commendation. Instead, though, he anticipates criticism and imagines every negative detail of what might happen.

Sam's situation is even more troublesome. Years ago his

wife, Louise, had a brief infatuation with one of his friends. Fortunately, she saw very soon what was happening and put an end to it. But Sam can't forget, and after all this time he still tortures himself with thoughts of the other men his wife might be attracted to. Nothing could be further from Louise's mind, but Sam's irrational jealousy is eating away at their marriage.

Often our imagination projects negative pictures of our future.

Stanley, a United Airlines captain, will be sixty years old in fourteen months. Until recently he was looking forward to the mandatory retirement age, but in the past few months his inner feelings have alarmed him. Imagining life without the excitement of demanding flight schedules and the bustle of huge airports brings on periods of depression.

Finally Stanley talked to a psychologist. "What's happening to me? I'm frightened of being sixty. I dread retirement. Am I going crazy?" he wanted to know. His imagination is robbing him of the excitement and adventure God may have ahead for him.

To a greater or lesser degree, we all face the problem of controlling the fear-producing power of our imaginations. As Emerson wrote:

> Some of your hurts you have cured
> And the sharpest you still have survived
> But what torment of grief you've endured
> From hurts that never arrived.

Unfortunately, enough hurts have arrived to intensify our fears about present problems. Bad memories tend to poison our imagination. Past fears multiplied by present anxieties equal a fearful imagination. When we brought our hurtful memories of the past to the Lord for healing (step number four), we were laying the groundwork for this next liberating step to living without fear.

Step number nine: *I confess my fearful imagination and today I ask the Lord through His Spirit to make my imagination a channel of His vision and not a breeding place of fear.*

In taking this step, it is important that we understand what the Lord intended our imaginations to be and how we frustrate and distort His original purpose. Then we can claim His power to live out each day as fearless, imaginative, and healthy Christians.

Imagination: Two Distorted Views

Before we examine how the transformation of our fear-filled imaginings can take place, we need to recognize and avoid two distorted views of the imagination that plague some Christians. And I don't believe that either of these views can be supported by Scripture.

First, there are those who refuse to believe that the imagination is a God-given gift. People who hold this view have somehow twisted things around to where they see the imagination as unreal and sinful.

This idea, in part at least, finds its roots in a confusion that arose when the Hebrew Old Testament was first translated into a Greek version known as the Septuagint. In a number of places the Hebrew word for "stubbornness" was translated into a Greek word that was used for the functions of the imagination.

Following that lead, the King James Version uses the English word "imagination" to translate the Hebrew word for "stubbornness." The New King James Version keeps the word "imagination" in most of the texts, but it clearly indicates in footnotes and margin notations that the word is "stubbornness" in the original Hebrew. The Revised Standard Version corrects the problem. For example, in the King James Version we read, "But they hearkened not, nor inclined their ear, but walked in the counsels and in the *imagination* of their evil heart, and went backward, and not forward" (Jer. 7:24, italics mine). Notice the difference in the Revised Standard Version, "But they did not obey or incline their ear, but walked in their own counsels and the *stubbornness* of their evil hearts, and went backward and not forward" (italics mine). Other examples are found in Deuteronomy 29:19, Jeremiah 9:14, 11:8, 13:10, 16:12, 18:22, and 23:17. From these examples you can see that if a person did not understand what had happened, it might be possible to equate the word "imagination" with evil and sinfulness.

The other distorted view of God's purpose for the imagination is called "image-theology." People who cling to this simplistic idea believe that all they need to do is identify their needs and wants, then name them before God and claim the results.

Many who hold this point of view back it up by asserting that God is anxious to give us whatever we want. But that idea misses a crucial first step—we first need God's guidance in seeing what we should really need and want. The wisdom writer put it this way: "Trust in the Lord with all your heart, and lean not on your own understanding; in all your ways acknowledge Him, and He shall direct your paths" (Prov. 3:5–6). If we fail to ask God's guidance and simply imagine what we want and demand that God produce it, we are well on our way to indulging in self-centered pride and the presumption of putting ourselves in a position of authority over God.

The element that is missing in image-theology is seeking guidance from God about what we should ask for. At the same time image-theology fails to consider God's methods and timing. There's much more involved than the pagan notion that to have or be anything we want, we merely need to form a picture of it in our minds and then act as if it had already happened.

Now, if we are to overcome both of the distorted views we have just looked at, we need to move on to examine

God's gift of imagination. Putting it to its intended use will rule out our misapplying it and allowing it to be a seedbed for the germination and growth of our fears.

God's Gift of Imagination

The imagination is the God-given ability of the thinking brain to form and hold images of thought. It is the drama department of the mind, giving our ideas form and structure. It produces the motion picture version of our thought. With the imagination we form the image of who we are, we envision what our lives can be, and we work out solutions to our problems. Our imagination is God's magnificent gift to us that opens the way to creativity, inventiveness, artistry, problem-solving, and visionary leadership.

Most important of all, the imagination is one of the most vital points of contact with the Lord's Spirit. It is a beachhead or entry point for the invasion of His Spirit into our inner being. God gave us the ability to imagine so that He could implant His purpose and plan in our minds and help us discover His will for us.

But sadly, like our other abilities, our imaginations became flawed and distorted when sin entered the world through the disobedience of Adam and Eve. It became a means for developing our thoughts of rebellion and pride instead of being a channel for the Lord's vision and guidance. Our separation from Him resulted in our thought life being the target of Satan and the imagination becoming vulnerable to the influence of evil. God's own analysis of our plight was, "The imagination of man's heart is evil from his youth" (Gen. 8:21).

But God was faithful in His love and care for His fallen creation. He chose Israel to be His people through whom He would demonstrate His power and love. Then He called leaders and used their fallible imaginations in which to form the vision of His plan for His people.

The Old Testament biographies of these leaders are amazingly honest. They are accounts of human response and resistance, success and failure.

In these stories we see how patient God was in working with His people. In almost all of the heroes and heroines of ancient Israel we find a startling mixture of the use and misuse of the imagination in cooperating with God or in rebelling against Him.

Leaders like Abraham, Moses, Joshua, Gideon, Saul, David, Solomon, Elijah, and Jonah, were men with vivid imagination and clear vision. They accomplished great things when God was in control. But their stories also reveal the passionate struggle each had between God's vision and their human willfulness.

There were times when the imagination of Israel's leaders was captured and enlivened by the Spirit of God, but their followers were dull and slow to respond because of their failure to catch the spark of God in their imaginations. The checkered history of their murmurings, rebellion, worship of other gods, and self-justifying legalism resulted in the most difficult periods of ancient Israel's history.

Christ and Imagination

The Good News found in our New Testament is that Jesus Christ, Author of life, through whom all things came to redeem all the functions of our minds and to transform our total nature. Throughout His ministry He appealed to the imagination, honoring its function to form, hold, and achieve images.

By His use of moving parables, incisive metaphors, and stirring allegories, Christ chose to *show* His message of truth rather than simply tell it. He imprinted on people's imaginations the picture of what life was meant to be, the true meaning of His kingdom, and the joy of abundant and

eternal life. His word pictures were so vivid that His followers were able to remember them years later and under the
guidance of the Spirit preserve them in the Gospels.

A New Creation

But Christ did not come just to awaken the imagination of
His hearers. He came to begin a new creation. His death
and resurrection brought salvation to every part of our nature. Nothing was left out. And when we invite Him to live
in us, the primary focus of His transforming work breaks
the stranglehold of fear and liberates the imagination to be
a servant of His Spirit in us.

A Promise for the Imagination

In Christ's death and resurrection and the outpouring of
the Spirit at Pentecost, the promise given through Joel became a reality. "And it shall come to pass afterward," says
God, "that I will pour out My Spirit on all flesh; your sons
and daughters shall prophesy, your old men shall dream
dreams, your young men shall see visions and also on My
menservants and on My maidservants I will pour out
My Spirit in those days" (2:28–29). This is not only the
prediction of what happened with the coming of the Spirit
at Pentecost, but is also the promise of the re-creation of the
imagination.

One of the most astounding contrasts of history is the
difference Pentecost and the infilling of Christ's Spirit
made in the imaginations of Jesus' disciples. Prior to His
death and resurrection and being anointed with His Spirit,
the disciples were fearful, vacillating, dull men who just
couldn't understand what Christ was saying. After Pentecost it all made sense to them, and what they were to be and
do was unmistakably clear. With Christ-filled imaginations
they exemplified the new creation He had called them to

experience and live. With the image of Christ as the focus of their imaginations, they grew in His likeness. Their fears were no longer exaggerated by their imaginations, but His promises were turned into specific hope for their own lives and what He would do through them.

An Anointed Imagination

Now, our imaginations are transformed when Christ anoints us with His Spirit. Our part in receiving His anointing is to confess the fears that dominate our imaginations and to ask for the panic-dispelling anointing of His Spirit. Just as His perfect love casts out fear of judgment, so too His indwelling Spirit captivates our thoughts in our imaginations and works to reshape them so we can picture His plan for our lives.

Christ wants to give us a new self-image—a vision of ourselves filled with His Spirit and completely under His control. Then He wants to dramatize in our imaginations what He is able to do in our problems and in our relationships. We are actually able to see Him at work in our troublesome situations.

What James Weldon Johnson prayed for the preacher in "Listen Lord" should become our daily, moment-by-moment prayer for ourselves.

> Put his eye to the telescope of eternity,
> And let him look upon the paper walls of time.
> Lord, turpentine his imagination,
> Fill him full of the dynamic of thy power,
> Anoint him all over with the oil of thy salvation,
> And set his tongue on fire.[1]

Turpentining the Imagination

The anointing of the Spirit of Christ acts like turpentine on our varnished imaginations. Many of us who believe in

Christ as Lord and Savior still have imaginations that are layered with the negative varnish of reserve and caution. Years of seeing reality only with our limited potential have encrusted our imaginations with memories of our weaknesses and failures. As a result, all we can picture with our imaginations is a repetition of the frightening things we've always had to endure.

But when we ask the Lord to captivate our imaginations, He does what turpentine does to the layered varnish and paint on a piece of wood. He softens the hard layers, scraping them off until our imagination is clean and can be penetrated by His Spirit. Only then can our imaginations become instruments of receiving His guidance in vivid, dramatized images of His plans for us.

It's All in Your Imagination

We've heard those five words, "It's all in your imagination," all through our lives. That saying has been used to convince us that our fears were hallucinations or self-deceptions. Our fears were dismissed as absurd and exaggerated.

Actually, the saying is accurate, but not in the ways it's customarily used. I want to say "It's all in your imagination" with a different meaning—stressing the importance of the imagination rather than ridiculing it.

All thought is processed by imagination. That's why a Christ-anointed imagination is so vital. Without that liberating gift our worst ideas of frightening possibilities will be aggravated and intensified.

The circuit between our imagination and our emotions and body systems will be activated. Powerful feelings of fear will pump adrenalin into our bloodstream. Inordinate stress will result. Many people live in that agitated state most of the time.

The only way to reverse the process is, indeed, all in our imaginations. And Christ can do it. When we surrender our imaginations to His control, He actually blocks some fears from even entering them. Others He reorients by showing us how He will be bringing good out of troublesome situations. Most of all, He keeps our imaginations so busy picturing what He wants us to be and do that there's little time left to look for new things to worry about.

The Lord wants to set us free to focus on His strategy for our lives, families, and churches. We can't serve Him effectively if we are crippled with a fearful imagination. And yet, He waits for us to ask for the transforming miracle of His anointing of our imaginations.

My Personal Experience

I can vividly remember the time, early in my ministry, when I first prayed for the anointing of Christ on my own imagination. A disturbing question had kept tumbling around in my mind. Why was I, and why were most of the people in my church, paralyzed by fear? We all lived in two worlds: our outer world of challenges and opportunities and our inner world of hidden fears. Though we believed in Christ, there was little evidence of boldness and courage as we confronted our problems.

As individuals we were worried and cautious. As participants in the church we were fearfully bound to the securities of our sober doctrines and cherished traditions. Vision and vitality were lacking.

In my search for answers I kept tripping over the biblical phrase "the fullness of God." Paul's prayer for the Ephesians alerted me to what I might be missing. "That Christ may dwell in your hearts through faith; that you, being rooted and grounded in love, may be able to comprehend with all the saints what is the width and length and depth and

height—to know the love of Christ which passes knowledge; that you may be filled with all the fullness of God"
(Eph. 3:17–19).

As I reflected on these words, I came to see how little of
God's fullness I had really experienced. Intellectual acceptance had not carried over into a vibrant and alive vision for
myself and the church.

So I asked myself, "If I have been created to receive all of
the fullness, have I responded with all of my life?" I thought
about the faculties the Lord had given me: intellect, memory, emotion, will. These I had rigorously tried to commit to
the Lord. And yet, something was missing that kept me
from linking what I believed to the life that I was actually
living. And fearfulness filled that void.

Marshaling Thought into Action

One day during my prayer and Bible study, a question
came to mind. What about my imagination? I had to admit
that I had never thought of including my imagination in my
commitment to the Lord. That realization moved me into a
profound study of the imagination.

It was then that I came to some firm convictions about the
power of the imagination. We are all in the process of becoming the person we imagine ourselves to be. How we see
ourselves in imagination will be the person we become.
The imagination is the marshaling faculty of the mind that
puts thought into action. It unifies our will, emotions, and
physical energies toward the accomplishment of the picture
it forms.

Also, I began to realize how our imaginations affect other
people. We can limit or liberate what they become by the
image we hold of them in our minds. If we picture other
people as if they don't count, that's what they will become
for us. They will probably fulfill our expectations of them.

Next, I want to picture the vital role of the imagination in the making of our plans and in the development of our expectations for the future. Just as we become the persons we imagine, so, too, our families, churches, companies, and community organizations are radically affected by the vision we have for what they can become.

It was at this point that I began to realize that I was using my imagination to promote fear and not faith. I saw that I desperately needed Christ's healing of my imagination.

In response to my need, I made a deep commitment of my imagination to the Lord and prayed for the fullness of His Spirit to fill it, heal it, and use it to help me see myself, other people, and the church the way He does. It was one of the turning points of my life.

The results were amazing. A few weeks after praying that prayer, I was delighted to realize that many of my persistent fears had not come back to mind. And when new fears surfaced, I claimed the Lord's healing and transformation of them. I began to pray, "Lord, help me imagine people as You see them." And I found new power to affirm their potential.

A Vision for the Church

The Lord also helped me see my church not as a religious institution but as a laboratory of new life in which people could meet Him and be filled with His power. New vision for the program of the church sparked my mind. My studies of the Scripture became much more exciting as I actually lived in the biblical scenes and passages, imagining what really had happened. Next, my preaching became an adventure. The Lord helped me to picture my listeners living out the truth that I had to share.

As I shared the secret of what I had discovered about the healing of the imagination in the overcoming of fear, many of my listeners identified with me in the need of the Lord to anoint their imaginations.

In countless conversations and counseling sessions about

their fears, I prayed specifically for the healing of their imaginations. The Lord answered these prayers by giving people a new picture of what He was willing, ready, and able to do in the very situations and relationships which were causing them fear.

Many of the people who experienced new vision for their personal lives were also leaders in the congregation. Together we began to pray, "Lord, liberate our imaginations. Help us to picture Your boldest, most adventuresome vision for the life and program of the church."

Board meetings and planning sessions began to change from dull, business-as-usual to very adventuresome times of vision. Our prayers continued, "Lord, what do You want? Transform our imaginations so we can dream Your dream. Paint the picture vividly in our thoughts and help us to move forward with You to accomplish Your vision by Your power and provision."

From all of this, you can see that my initial discovery of the power of a Christ-motivated imagination had a profound impact on my life and ministry. But that was only the beginning. It has had to be renewed every day so that I can live without fear and boldly grasp the Lord's vision.

The Secret Place

Like the psalmist, I must retreat to a "secret place" for daily renewal. It's a place where I am able to meet the Lord and listen to Him. He is waiting there for us. The psalmist knew about that place.

> He who dwells in *the secret place* of the Most High
> Shall abide under the shadow of the Almighty.
> I will say of the Lord, "He is my refuge and my fortress;
> My God, in Him I will trust" (Ps. 91:1–2, italics mine).

The Hebrew word for "secret place" really means "shelter"— a place of protection and refuge.

The same idea is expressed in the Twenty-third Psalm:

"You prepare a table before me in the presence of my enemies." In the psalmist's time, if you could reach the tent or dwelling of a friend and sit down at his table, you would not be attacked by your enemies as long as you remained in the protecting presence of your host. For us, that place of refuge is the heart of God.

Jesus said, "Let not your heart be troubled; you believe in God, believe also in Me. In My Father's house are many mansions; if it were not so, I would have told you. I go to prepare a place for you. And if I go and prepare a place for you, I will come again and receive you to Myself; that where I am, there you may be also" (John 14:1–3).

I believe more is involved in Jesus' words than preparation of a place in heaven for us after we die. Rather, I am convinced that He meant He was going to Calvary to prepare a place for us in the heart of God, a place of love, forgiveness, reconciliation, and healing. Surely, that's what is implied by His promise that He would come again and receive us to Himself, that where He is we may be also.

And so we ask, where is He now? He is with us to lead us into the mansions, the resting places of the Father's house now—daily, hourly. That's our "secret place" to which we can retreat for the reformation of our imaginations. It's there that our fearful thoughts in our imaginations are changed into images of hope. It is there that our perception of what might happen is exchanged for the Lord's picture of what He has planned for us.

I could not live without these visits to the secret place of the Most High. There, repeatedly, I commit my imagination to be an agent of the Lord's thought for me and my needs. I spread out before the Lord the real and perceived fears that are hassling me. Then the Lord gives me the picture of the person He wants me to be in both character and personality. He shows me His image of what He wants me to do and say in my relationships. And I receive His vision of people to replace my inadequate expectations for them.

The Apostle Paul gives us a vivid description of what can happen to the imagination in the secret place when he writes, "Eye has not seen, nor ear heard, nor have entered into the heart of man the things which God has prepared for those who love Him" (1 Cor. 2:9). The Apostle goes on to make this astounding statement. "But God has revealed them to us through His Spirit" (2:10).

Then what follows is an exciting explanation of how the Spirit, who knows the deep things of God and the depths of our needs for the inspiration of our imaginations, actually guides our thoughts, ". . . that we might know the things that have been freely given to us by God" (2:12). And a little further on Paul adds, "For 'who has known the mind of the Lord that He may instruct Him?' But we have the mind of Christ" (2:16). That is awesome! The Greek word for "mind" used here has the meaning "intelligence." What Paul is actually saying here is that we are offered the divine intelligence of Christ as the source of the images formed in our imaginations.

How It Works

In another favorite passage from Paul, we discover how the creative use of imagination works in the secret place. "The Lord is at hand. Be anxious for nothing, but in everything by prayer and supplication, with thanksgiving, let your requests be made known to God; and the peace of God, which surpasses all understanding, will guard your hearts and minds through Christ Jesus" (Phil. 4:5b–7).

Christ is not only coming back again, but He is present with us now. He takes us by the hand and leads us into the secret place. There our anxious thoughts and fears can be spread out before the Lord in prayer, supplication, and thanksgiving.

Prayer, in this context, means calling upon the Lord and claiming His presence and power. We approach the Lord by telling Him who He is to us. He is *Jehovah-Shammah,* the Lord ever-present; *Jehovah-Rapha,* the Lord our healer; *Jehovah-Shalom,* the Lord our peace. All this we know in and through His Son, Christ our Lord, Immanuel, God with us. Christ is the heart of God meeting our frightened hearts with love.

In confident trust we can offer our prayers. We can tell the Lord our problems and perplexities. We do that with thanksgiving. As we thank Him for the things that have driven us to the secret place of prayer we not only remember the Lord's goodness in the past, but fully submit our present needs to Him. Thanksgiving is the ultimate and final act of submission; we are not completely free of our difficulties until we have thanked the Lord for them and for His wisdom in allowing them.

Now, our imaginations become open to the pictures of what He wants to do only after we pray, "Lord, thank You for these problems. I praise You that You have chosen me to be a channel for implementing the divine solutions You will help me imagine. I trust my imagination totally to You and will live out the vision You have given to me."

Only then does peace replace our panic. Paul says that peace actually guards our hearts and minds. Christ *is* our peace (Eph. 2:14, italics mine). He stands as the sentinel of our imaginations, holding off any invasion of fear that might disturb our sure vision of what we have been guided to do or be. His peace-infusing presence also helps us each step of the way in making the vision a reality.

In Colossians 3:15, Paul speaks of peace ruling in our hearts. The Greek word translated "rule" also means "umpire." God's peace, indwelling in Christ, calls the plays, showing what is right or wrong for us to do. He not only guards the entrance of our imaginations, He rules out things we might think of doing that will entrap us in further fear.

My friend Paul Baskin has experienced that. He's an out-

standing contemporary Christian songwriter. I was profoundly moved by hearing him sing his song "The Secret
Place." The last verse summarizes what happens to the
imagination in the secret place of intimate prayer.

> In the secret place
> I see Your beauty
> In the secret place
> My thoughts are healed
> For You are Lord, You are Lord
> I will not be ashamed
> I will not be afraid
> For in Your likeness I'm made
> In the secret place.[2]

Faith and Imagination

It is there, deep in the secret place, that the gifts of imagination and faith work together to overcome our fears. Our
responsibility is to seek to know the Lord's will. It is His
responsibility to implant in our yielded imaginations the
clear, impelling vision of what He wants to do for and
through us. Then He gives us the gift of faith to trust Him.

As the author of Hebrews puts it, "Now faith is the sub-
stance of things hoped for, the evidence of things not seen"
(Heb. 11:1). We realize in our mind's eye what we are to
pray for with confidence and assurance. Actually, growing
in faith is dependent on ever-increasing, fresh inspiration
of our imagination.

Get-the-Picture Charlie

Recently, on a trip to North Carolina, I ran into an old
friend. He has a speech habit that has earned him the name
"Get-the-picture Charlie." Charlie is a great talker. His
monologues are laced with colorful southern colloquial-
isms, metaphors, and allegories. But his desire to be under-

stood prompts him to punctuate his seemingly endless flow of words with "Get the picture?"

Though the Lord never tires us with endless words, He is urgently concerned that we "get the picture" of His plan for our lives and of His specific guidance in the fearful problems of our daily living.

Now, to recap, here are the vital elements of this ninth step in living without fear.

1.   Thank the Lord for the gift of imagination. Praise Him that by His grace it is possible to picture your life filled with the Lord's love, joy, and peace.

2.   Confess to Him the ways you may have misused the gift and developed a fearful imagination.

3.   Claim the truth that He died on the cross for the redemption of all your faculties including your imagination.

4.   Specifically ask for the anointing of His Spirit on your imagination.

5.   Spread out your fears before the Lord and ask Him to transform your fearful picture of what might happen into a vision of what He wills for you to do and be in those very situations.

6.   Visit the secret place of intimate communion with the Lord at the beginning and end of each day and repeatedly throughout the day. Each time a new fear attacks, go there immediately for His perspective, peace, and power.

Step 10 _____

I will face my eventual physical death
and claim that I am alive eternally.
Therefore, I can live abundantly
without panic
for the rest of my time on earth.

_____

Fast-Forward to the Beginning

AMY HARWELL HAS EVERY REASON TO WANT TO LIVE A FULL and long life. She's a brilliant, talented, attractive young woman with a successful career as a speech consultant to business leaders. And yet, Amy has been diagnosed as having cancer with a grim prognosis for the future.

I met Amy recently when I was in Chicago to speak on the Chicago "Sunday Evening Club" television program. She gave her witness as part of the program and spoke with clarity, power, and joy about what Christ had done in her life and how He was helping her face the agony of a very uncertain future. I will never forget how Amy in her witness that night, answered the question, "How has your faith helped you handle your problems?"

The Healing of Brokenness

"Well, quite frankly," Amy said, "for thirty-three years my life was smooth sailing—very smooth—almost as if I lived on a luxury cruise ship. But then the storms came. Literally, my life began to break apart. In the past three years, I've had a broken heart, a broken body, and as a result of those two, a broken bank account. And during one of my 'breaks' I felt unlovable.

"With reference to my broken heart, I felt unlovable because I was literally told by someone very important to me, 'I don't love you anymore.'

"And regarding my body, my treatment for cancer included four trips to the operating room, fifty radiation treatments, a radiation implant requiring isolation, and thirty days of twenty-four-hour chemotherapy.

"I felt lonely and unattractive. Now I can neither conceive nor adopt a child. And with such a prognosis, who would want to love or marry me?

"The costs of treatment almost broke my finances. When self-support was difficult for a time, I found it hard to maintain self-esteem.

"I asked my doctor, 'How many of your patients have lived to the magic five-year mark with my type and spread of cancer?' His answer was, 'No one.'

"I needed a friend. During each of my 'breaks' two songs from my youth camp days crept into my head repeatedly— 'Jesus Loves Me' and 'What a Friend We Have in Jesus.' Well, certainly, Jesus qualified to be a friend, but where was He? Did I have to wait for Him to come down from the clouds or in a miraculous event if I could stretch my faith? I needed Him then!

"I discovered that I didn't need to look to the sky. In addition to His own presence, He came to me in my parents and friends. You see, when I was broken, Jesus loved me through my family and friends—through His church, the body of Christ. He cheered, sustained, and came to me through them. He gave me peace through their eye contact, hope through their smiles, and joy through their touch."

Amy went on to explain the power of the prayers of friends in healing her brokenness. Through these prayers and moving experiences of Christ's power in healing services at an Episcopal church in Geneva, Illinois, finally she was able to surrender to Christ her illness and fear of dying.

After hearing this remarkable young woman speak on the program, I had a good visit with her. I wanted to know more specifically how Christ had helped Amy overcome her fear of sickness and death. She used a moving metaphor in her radiant reply.

"Lloyd," she said confidently, "when I was given my final prognosis, it was as if someone had pushed the fast-forward button on my videotape machine. I couldn't help playing through the tape to the probable end of the scene. Often we speak of fast-forwarding a videotape to the end. For me, facing my death and knowing I am alive forever was like fast-forwarding to the beginning!

"I'm not afraid of death anymore. In fact, panic over sickness is gone. However long I live physically matters so much less now, and I'm really free to live now and forever."[1]

Fast-Forward to the Beginning

A fast-forward to the beginning! That's exactly what I pray this chapter will be for you and me. I want to speed up the videotape of our lives in our minds to our own dying. And, like Amy, I'm convinced that the experience, when done in the full assurance of Christ's victory over death, will be a liberating release from the fear of sickness and dying. We'll discover that claiming death as a transition in living—a new beginning, and not an end—will be the start of a wonderful freedom to live more fully now and for however long we have left on this earth.

Talk of Death Can Be Frightening

You may find that talking about death is threatening. Most of us don't like to think about our dying, much less talk about it.

On her seventy-ninth birthday Bette Davis was interviewed on the "Today" show by Bryant Gumbel. She expressed her curiosity about her mortality. "I'm really
curious about how I will go and what will happen. But my
friends don't like it when I talk about it. 'Don't talk about it,'
they say. 'We don't want to hear about it.'"

Even writing our wills can be an unsettling experience. We
are part of a society that abhors aging and is constantly in
search of cosmetics, therapeutic vitamins, diets, and health
kicks to keep us looking young.

At the same time there is a frenzy about exposing things
we eat or do that are not good for our health. And each new
discovery about health problems sends most of us into a
hypochondriacal tailspin, worrying that we may have the
latest strain of virus or flu, or that we may be candidates for
some new type of cancer. This panic is only a symptom of
our greater fear of death.

We all want to live a full and healthy physical life as long
as we can. "And why not?" you may protest.

We love living. The thought of physical suffering, in
whatever grotesque form it may take before we die, is ab-
horrent to us. And the possibility of an untimely accidental
death is equally alarming. Most of us have made our plans
for the years ahead. Thinking about leaving loved ones,
friends, and the things we've accumulated to enjoy is not
only unpleasant, but excruciating. There's so much to do,
see, and experience. Lurking beneath our gusto for living is
the grief we harbor about dying.

Unfortunately, many Christians, who should have the
greatest freedom from the fear of death, are often no more
confident than nonbelievers. We want Christ to help us live
the abundant life now, but we give far too little thought to
our eternal life. And often when we are hit with sickness
ourselves or face it in our loved ones, we find that the
extent of our faith is our hope that Christ will intervene to
heal us so that we can live longer. We lust for a long life.

Quantity of years becomes more important than the quality of our lives. Since we try to think about death as little as possible, our faith is not stretched to include a vibrant confidence that whether we live or die, we belong to the Lord.

But the fear of sickness and death still lurks beneath the surface of our minds. An illness or the death of a loved one or friend forces us to think about death, and then we submerge this disturbing subject again and race on in the fast lane of living.

A Bold Step to Overcome the Fear of Death

Overcoming the fear of death, like all the other fears we've considered, takes place when we confront it and take a bold step in our twelve-step strategy of living without fear. Step number ten: *I will face my eventual physical death and claim that I am alive eternally. Therefore, I can live abundantly without panic for the rest of my time on earth.*

The promise of Scripture I want to claim for this very crucial step honestly recognizes what the fear of death does to us and states what Christ has done about this life-sapping anguish. In 1 Corinthians 15:25–26 we are reminded that we can be free of the first fear of the last enemy. "For He [Christ] must reign till He has put all enemies under His feet. The last enemy that will be destroyed is death."

This verse boldly affirms the reigning, triumphant Christ's victory over death. It also realistically recognizes that fear of death is still a formidable enemy for us. In the interval between Christ's resurrection and His return, physical illness and death will confront us. But through the miracle of our own personal, spiritual resurrection now and our regeneration into new people in Christ, we can know with assurance that our physical dying will be only a transition in the onward flow of our eternal life. Let's talk about how that happens.

Christ's Victory

The conquest of the fear of death begins with Christ's death and resurrection. That's not just "Easter talk." It is the central fact that sparks faith and provides the solid reason for assurance. The pre-existent Christ, the One through whom all things were made, the Author of life, the creating power of God, lived among us as Life in all its fullness. He who said, "I have come that they may have life and that they may have it more abundantly," and "I am the way, the truth, and the life," is the same Lord who suffered on the cross for our forgiveness and rose from the dead as victor over the power of death.

As the author of Hebrews summarizes so movingly, "Inasmuch then as the children have partaken of flesh and blood, He Himself likewise shared the same, that through death He might destroy him who had the power of death, that is the devil, and release those who through fear of death were all their lifetime subject to bondage" (Heb. 2:14–15).

That raises a question. The writer of Hebrews speaks of Christ's victory as finished. But Paul says that Christ must reign until He has put all enemies under His feet, and that the last enemy to be destroyed will be death. Does that mean that Christ's victory over death is incomplete?

Not at all. Christ reigns as Lord to love us, to give us the gift of faith in Him, and to enable us to claim His triumphant defeat of death by rising from the dead. His resurrection is our personal assurance that death holds no power over us. It's more than an idea we accept; it's an experience that can transform us.

For that, we need a firsthand experience of the presence of the resurrected, living Lord and a personal realization that because He lives we also shall live now and forever. No secondhand experience of the Easter miracle will give us freedom from the fear of death.

A Secondhand Easter

There's a secondhand store in Hollywood, California, that touts the resale of the wardrobes of the stars. For a price, you can buy, wear, and pretend you have the charisma of your favorite star of stage and screen. At least, that's the sizzle of the store's advertising.

Recently, during Holy Week, I drove by the shop and was amazed by a sign in the window. In bold letters it read, "Have a firsthand Easter with a secondhand Easter bonnet worn by a star!" I could hardly believe my eyes. Someone had spent a lot of time on the wording of that eye-catching sign!

You can imagine the seed of thought that sign planted in the furrows of my mind. It takes more than a secondhand hat worn by a celebrity, or even a new one, to have a firsthand Easter. The sign started me thinking about the kind of an Easter that would be "firsthand" all year long. It is one in which we meet the risen Lord personally.

Actually, a secondhand experience will not be sufficient for our firsthand encounter with the fear of sickness and death. Rumored hope, hearsay faith from others, and inherited tradition won't help us when we come to grips with our physical limitations and mortality.

A Test of Firsthand Hope

A good way to test how much of a firsthand experience we have had with the risen Lord and the power of His resurrection is to think and feel through how we would react if we were told that we had only one month left to live.

Would our relationship with Christ give us the courage we would need? Would His victory over death be our assurance that in spite of our physical death we are alive forever? This fast-forwarding of the videotape of our lives to our death not only shows us our real attitude about our own dying, but reveals a lot about the level of our intimacy with Christ.

How Some Christians React

I asked a group of five hundred people at a retreat, most of them church members, to write on a card how they would feel if they were told they had a short time left to live physically.

Seventy-five said they were ready and felt that they were sure of their relationship with Christ and eternal life through Him.

Two hundred and twenty said, in a variety of ways, that the question had shocked them with how superficial their relationship with Christ really was and that they were not prepared to die.

One hundred and sixty said they would feel cheated because they had so much more they wanted to do. Forty expressed concern over those they would leave behind.

Eighty said they didn't know and the rest of the group expressed discomfort, anxiety, and even anger that I'd raised the question. Everything from, "I wished you hadn't asked!" to "It's none of your business!" was written by the people in this category.

The rest of the retreat was an intense time of encounter with Christ. He used the question to touch the raw nerve of our fear of death and our lack of assurance of eternal life. That assurance can come only as a result of a firsthand relationship with Him. I'm thankful that by the end of the retreat we had Easter and Pentecost all rolled into one on a Saturday afternoon in October!

Preparation for Death

Preparation for death begins now. And it's so much more than claiming Christ's victory over the grave. That's only the beginning. The greatest miracle of the living Lord is our resurrection, not just at the time of our physical death, but now. Without that, we are unprepared to die and unable to live triumphantly without fear.

Christ said, "I am the resurrection and the life. He who believes in Me, though he may die, he shall live. And whoever lives and believes in Me shall never die. Do you believe this?" (John 11:25–26).

Well, do you believe it? Yes, we say, but often in a vague way that does little to overcome our own panic about death. It is true that we claim Christ's promise when a loved one dies or when we are seriously ill. But often we are doing little more than clutching for immortality, and wishing that in some mysterious way our physical death won't be the end. But even with that, we loathe the eventuality of death. Why?

More Than Living Forever

A belief that we will live forever does little to overcome our fear of death because, if that is all we have, we are haunted with a deeper fear—where and how we will spend our forever. That's why repeated affirmation that death is not an ending really makes us more fearful. It's what might happen after death that makes dying so frightening. That's why to many the idea of immortality is meaningless. Life after death? Who wants to live forever?

Only those people for whom heaven has begun now want to live forever. For the Christian, eternal life is now, through the life, death, and resurrection of Jesus. His promise wasn't just to "live forever." Instead, He gave us life with both quality and quantity.

The Rock of Experience

There is no substitute for what John Henry Jowett, preacher and writer of prominence early in the twentieth

century, called "the rock of experience." We know only what
we have experienced. When we confront the enemy of death
there is no greater weapon than our own personal fellowship with the risen Lord. As He did battle with Satan and
peeled back the fingers of his stranglehold on humankind
with the grip of fear of death, so, too, He seals us with a
protective shield against Satan's influence over our thinking
and feeling.

Satan's strategy is to try to influence us with the false
idea that this life is all there is, that death is a horrible
ending, and that we really cannot be sure of the joy of
heaven. He tempts us with pride's silly idea that if we were
to die our loved ones could not make it without us, that our
hard work would be lost, and that our little world would
collapse. Satan tries to sentimentalize everything. We get
teary about the things we'll never get to touch again, favorite places we won't enjoy again, and pleasurable happen-
ings we won't delight in ever again.

But in fellowship with the Lord, we are set free to enjoy
life to the fullest, knowing that everything matters because
nothing ultimately matters except our relationship with
Him. As a part of loving Him we are free to love people more
profoundly than ever before, without demanding that they
be our reason for living. We can use things with great joy
without being dominated by the idea that we are what we
possess. Our work no longer is our god, the source of our
meaning and purpose. That releases us to work harder and
better without stress or burnout. We can live every day with
all stops out as if it were our last day on earth because we
know it's only one more day in forever.

Here's How It Works

Here's how Christ's promise works. Christ invades our
lives with the power of His grace. In countless ways, He
shows us that the life we are living is no life at all in compari-

son with abundant life in Him. He helps us admit that we are sinners, separated from God. Persistently and tenderly, Christ creates in us a profound sense of our emptiness and loneliness. Lovingly, He forces us to see what we are doing to hurt ourselves and others. He faces us with the disturbing truth that our arrogant efforts to run our own lives are failing. Not even our good works and achievements qualify us for status with God or assurance of eternal life.

It's usually some crisis that breaks our pride, some challenge that convinces us we don't have what it takes, or some opportunity that's beyond us, that forces us to admit our need for Christ. For some people, the need for Christ is realized at a time of failure. For others the need surfaces in response to the needs of people and the cultural plight of the world. For still others, the need for Christ is realized by the witness of Christians who are attempting honestly to live out their faith each day. The Lord will use whatever is necessary to break through our defenses and open us up to the reality of His love for us.

It is then that we begin to experience the joy in losing our lives being disciples of Jesus. And as His followers, we submit ourselves to His leadership in every decision because we want Him to be the absolute Lord of our lives.

The great good news of all times is that when we respond, accepting Him as our Savior *and* committing our lives to Him as Lord, we are resurrected out of an old life into a new life in Him. It's then that heaven begins. And with it comes the exciting process of regeneration.

Regeneration

Regeneration is rebirth and reformation. The Lord we've confessed must now become the indwelling power who conforms us to His image. We need a personal experience of Pentecost.

The well-known pastor and devotional writer F. B. Meyer

tells about the night it happened to him. He was walking in the Cumberland hills in solitude, with this prayer surging in his heart.

"If there is one soul more than any other within the circle of these hills who needs the gift of Pentecost, it is I: I want the Spirit, but I do not know how to receive Him; and I am too weak to think, or feel, or pray intensely."

Dr. Meyer heard an inner voice say: "As you took forgiveness from the hand of the dying Christ, take the gift of the Spirit from the hand of the living Christ." To this Meyer responded, "Lord, as I breathe in this whiff of warm night air, so I breathe into every part of me Your blessed Spirit!" Recounting his experience, Dr. Meyer said, "I took, and took for the first time, and I have been taking ever since."

When we invite Christ to abide in us, He takes up residence in our total being. From within, He shapes the new person we are destined to be. Intellect, imagination, emotions, and will come under His inspiring, repatterning influence. We have a new perspective, passion, and power. Christ gives us a new outgoing and loving personality, a new zest for living to the fullest, a new freedom to know and do His will.

Now that Christ-filled, unified, and healed person inside us is alive forever. Our physical bodies will age and grow weak. They will endure sickness and eventual termination. But the spiritual body—our mind, soul, and spirit—will live forever. As surely as Christ was raised from the tomb, so, too, our true self will be lifted out of our bodies to the next phase of the heaven that we began here on earth.

The Sure Cure of Fear

So, the only sure way to overcome the fear of death is to die! That's more than a clever play on words. When we surrender our lives to Christ, we die to ourselves. In the hymn "Hark the Herald Angels Sing," Charles Wesley joyfully proclaimed this truth: Christ was "born that man no more may die, born to raise the sons of earth, born to give them second birth."

Everyone who has experienced the second birth needs have no fear of the second death. Our first (spiritual) death happened when Christ was born in us. Our second (physical) death, whenever we leave our physical bodies behind, will be like going to sleep and awakening to our next day in heaven.

To Live Is Christ

In a magnificent way, Paul fast-forwarded the videotape of his life when he wrote to the Philippian Christians during his imprisonment in Rome, "With all boldness, as always, so now also Christ will be magnified in my body, whether by life or by death. For to me, to live is Christ, and to die is gain" (1:20b–21).

The Apostle really believed that death would be a gain, a fuller union with Christ. I am convinced that we cannot say, "For me to live is Christ," until we have said, and meant, "For to die is gain." When we have thought through our dying, we are ready for abundant living. No longer do we have to cling to the days and years of our physical life on earth as if they were all there is.

Mysterious as it may seem, an anticipation of heaven gives us a greater excitement about living now. Knowing that we are going to live forever frees us to live now with greater gusto.

Alexander Maclaren, the great nineteenth-century adventuresome communicator of eternal life, said that this is the "true anesthetic which will give us a 'solemn scorn of ills' and make even the last and greatest change from life to death of little account."

It's fascinating to note that after Paul affirmed that Christ was his life in dying or living, he could turn his attention more vibrantly to the needs of the Philippians. "Nevertheless to remain in the flesh is more needful for you. And being confident of this, I know that I shall remain and continue with you all for your progress and joy of faith, that your rejoicing for me may be more abundant in Jesus Christ by my coming to you again" (Phil. 1:24–26).

Our Two Priorities

Paul's peace about dying renewed his passion for his two priorities—Christ and the needs of people. Christ was not only his Savior and Lord, He was the very air he breathed, the pulsebeat of his passion, the captivating thought of every moment. Christ was the indwelling power of Paul's mind, emotions, and will. Having died to himself when he surrendered his life to Christ, he became a post-resurrection dwelling place of the Holy Spirit. A new man had been created in his inner being who could no more be ended by physical death than the grave could hold the crucified Lord Jesus. It was this assurance that gave Paul a courageous assertiveness, a bold audacity. And all of his passion for living was focused in his desire to care for the deepest needs in people—to meet and know Christ personally, and experience the confidence of eternal life. To Paul, physical death was little more than a transition to the next and greater stage of life in Christ.

A Passion for Living

The people I know who have put fear of death behind them have this same passion for living. No longer having to cram life into the brief years that will be carved on their gravestone, they live each day to the fullest because they know they are alive forever. And the distinguishing quality of their lives is that they really care about people. Relationships are their top priority. There's no frantic rush about them. They have time to listen, care, and enjoy people. After all, what's the hurry when you know you're living one more day in forever?

Grace for Gray Days

There's no better tonic for life's gray days than that! So many days for most people are gray, not bright with blessings or dark with bleakness, just gray with boredom. They endure the grayness in anticipation of some exciting event to invade the dullness, some new possession to capture their attention for a time, some thrilling trip to get away from it all. But this is not true for a Christian who can say, "To die is gain, for me to live is Christ." For the Christian, there's a relaxed purposefulness to all of life.

When John Wesley was asked what he would do if he knew that a particular day was his last, he responded with unfrenzied calm that he would read the Bible, pray his prayers, preach, and have tea with some friends: no different from most of his days. And yet, with that freedom from panic, Wesley traveled 225,000 miles, mostly on horseback, and preached 40,000 times until the day of his death.

Wesley's dying words were, "And best of all—Christ is with us." Then he went on to heaven for a continued realization of the fullness of Christ. But heaven had begun the day Wesley's heart was "strangely warmed" by the infilling of Christ's Spirit at Aldersgate. After that, all of his hardships, conflicts, and difficulties were taken in stride. The days of the earthly portion of Wesley's eternal life were anything but gray. They were filled with the brightness of Christ's presence.

Are there Christians like that today? Yes! And you and I are meant to be among them. We can live without a fear of death. It's all a matter of believing in the risen Christ, knowing Him firsthand, experiencing the power of His resurrection and regeneration in us, and beginning the joy of heaven now.

An Affirmation of Fearless Confidence

How can we be sure of a faith that wipes out all fear of death? I believe this happens as the following affirmations become a present reality in our lives:

"I believe in Jesus Christ as my Savior. He died on the cross for my sins to set me free of guilt and condemnation. I know that I am loved and forgiven. Old memories of failures and mistakes have been healed forever.

"I believe in Christ as my Lord. He rose from the dead and reigns as my victorious conqueror over death. He liberates me from the fear of death and all lesser fears. Now I can live with freedom and joy.

"I believe in Christ as indwelling power. He has promised that He will abide in me and I in Him. I invite Him to live in my mind, to think His thoughts through me, to take charge of my will, to guide me to do His will, and to control my emotions to love through me.

"I accept the awesome wonder that I am an Easter miracle. By grace, I have been resurrected from the graves of self-centeredness, worry, and anxiety—to live for others. Therefore, I commit my whole life to Christ and will seek to be His faithful and obedient disciple in all my relationships and responsibilities.

"For me to live is Christ! I am truly alive, now and forever. Hallelujah and amen."

Step 11 _____

Today, I commit myself
to motivating people with love
rather than manipulating them with fear.

_____

Motivating
with Love

DO YOU EVER GET FRUSTRATED WITH PEOPLE?

Who doesn't?

Getting people to do what we want, when we want it, and how we want it, can be very frustrating.

Trying to change people is even more exasperating. Especially when we think we know what's best for them. The things they do and say can infuriate us. And when we see them hurting themselves and others, we want to step in and straighten them out.

Often our impatience reaches a boiling point. It's then that we are tempted to manipulate people with fear. We threaten them with the withdrawal of affection or approval. The law of the jungle, retaliation, becomes our method of getting what we want. Soon we are issuing an ultimatum: "If you don't, I won't!" It's an evidence that we've failed to motivate people with love.

To be free of fear, we have to stop using it to get things to go our way. When we rely on fear to coerce people, it grows in us. The more fear we create in others, the more it tightens its stranglehold on us. That's why I have included this next vital step in our twelve steps of living without fear.

Step number eleven: *Today, I commit myself to motivating people with love rather than manipulating them with fear.*

We need to begin by understanding how we all manipulate with fear at times. Then we will be ready to consider how to become dynamic motivators with love.

To better understand how this works, you may find it helpful to picture in your mind's eye the people who frustrate you. Think of those you'd like to change, most of all. Chances are, they are the people closest to you, in your family, among your friends, or at your place of work. In fact, the closer people are to us, the greater our frustration over not being able to get them to march to the drumbeat of our desires.

Manipulation in Marriage

Manipulation with fear often happens in marriage. Many people spend a lifetime trying to transform their mates. Our spouse's habits, personality quirks, attitudes—along with bigger things like values and beliefs—can distress us. The "for better or for worse" phrase of the marriage vow becomes difficult to keep. Generally, the better we know our mate, the more the "worse" becomes the target of our reformation efforts.

Manipulation with fear is subtle at first. We call it bartering or negotiation. When that fails, many husbands or wives draw a hard line and say, "Do what I want or don't expect me to do what you want!" Sex often becomes a powerful ploy: "If you persist in doing what I've asked you to change, don't come to bed expecting any affection from me!"

But sex is not the only trump card. As soon as we discover what's really important to our mate, we have power. The possibility of withholding whatever that is becomes a manipulative device. And the ultimate manipulation with fear in marriage is, "If you don't change your ways, I'm going to leave!" And the counter-manipulation, "Don't bother. If anyone is going to leave, I'll be the first!"

Manipulating Children

Manipulation with fear is also used to get children to measure up. Raising a family can be frustrating. We want our kids to reach their full potential. That's usually defined in our own wishes and standards. Sometimes our kids imitate the worst in us and deny our best. We are alarmed by the first and infuriated by the second. And so, the weary task of reminding, scolding, cajoling, urging, goes on through the growing years. We barter privileges for performance. When that doesn't work, parents of teenagers often use fear of punishment or even teeter on the brink of disaster with, "Do it our way or get out!"

Fortunately, in most families manipulation with fear does not go that far. However, many people reach adulthood having been kept in line with less blatant threats. The tragedy is that most of them repeat the parental pattern of using fear to get others to perform. The lesson has been learned all too well. They've watched parents manipulate each other and have felt manipulated by fear themselves.

Manipulation Invades Friendships

Manipulating with fear can also invade our friendships. We all have some friends we'd like to shape up. We get impatient with their life-styles, what they think is important, or the way they treat others. We get angry when we can't get them to do what *we* think is best for them. Our attitude becomes, "Play the game my way or I won't play at all." Of course we seldom express it with that crassness; we're just "busy" when they call, or we draw a social circle and exclude them.

On the Job

At work, manipulation often crowds out motivation. If we have people working for us, we face the constant challenge of defining goals, clarifying expectations, and inspiring excellence. Working for others is not a bed of roses either, especially if we think we could do their jobs better. But even if we're not bucking for their jobs, getting them to conform to our specifications can give us sleepless nights, if not high blood pressure. "If only they would do things our way!" we mutter.

For some managers, the spiked club of firing people if they don't perform keeps some workers on their toes. But employees have long known the power of uncooperativeness or divisiveness or going over a boss's head with a juicy slice of confidential information about his or her ineptness.

The power struggle goes on, and beneath the surface is manipulation with fear.

A Personal Inventory

Pause for a moment and consider ways you have felt manipulated with fear in the realms of marriage, family, friendships, or work. Perhaps the manipulation was not communicated by a direct confrontation, but it was there nonetheless. Unless I miss my guess, it's happened often. You have felt victimized and pushed around with threats, however veiled they may have been.

Now, I want to ask a personal question. Can you identify any relationship in which you are a manipulator rather than a motivator? Strange as it may seem, even when we know how much we abhor being manipulated by fear, we still use it to get others to be or do what we want—often with the best intentions.

Scare the Hell out of Him!

Recently, Richard talked to me about a man he wanted to help. His frustration was at the explosion point. "How do you intend to change this man?" I asked. His reply was one we've all been tempted to express at times. He said, "I'm going to scare the hell out of him and put the fear of God into him!"

Having tried that a few times in my own efforts to help people, I was quick to caution my friend that it wouldn't work. "You can frighten the man, but I doubt whether scaring him will change the 'hell' he's living in, and threatening him with God's judgment will not give him the power to be different. Why not try to put the love of God into him by sharing how God's love has helped you to change? Tell me, how has God helped you?"

My friend's stern, judgmental attitude softened. He could remember two big changes in his life. One was when his doctor told him he was going to have a heart attack unless he changed his life-style and lost fifty pounds.

"Did the doctor try to scare the 'hell' out of you?" I asked.

"No," the man responded. "He had been my confidant and trusted advisor for years and he gave me the prognosis with great empathy and concern."

"Then, how did you lose all the weight?" I queried.

In reply, he told me about meeting with a group of people in our church who encouraged each other to lose weight. He said they were his "cheering section." It was encouragement and love—not fear—that had given my friend victory in his battle to change his eating habits.

The other big change in this man's life had come in his marriage. One day a few years ago, his wife honestly confessed that she was really hurting in their marriage as it was. "How about her?" I asked. "Did she scare the 'hell' out of you?" My friend smiled knowingly, indicating that he was getting the point.

"Not at all," he said reflectively. "In fact, it was her willingness to admit her part in our problems that opened me up to want to get help together. And now we've got a better marriage than ever."

The brief review of how changes had taken place in his own life drained out the anger he was feeling and gave him a desire to encourage the man he had wanted to blast.

Strange, isn't it . . . how easily we all forget how people motivated us with love and fall back on manipulating others with fear.

Another friend of mine has faced how he was manipulating his wife to get what he wanted. He has realized how much fear has dominated his life and relationships.

A few weeks ago he told me, "My motto for people has been, 'If you screw up, you're history.' With that I could usually keep people in line. I never felt close to anyone, but most of the time I got what I demanded. What I didn't want was a wife who was frightened of me, but that's exactly what I produced. Talk about screwing up! I almost crushed a lovely person!"

Getting What We Don't Want

It's true—when we use fear to get what we want, we end up with what we don't want—acquiescence, compliance, and a lot of pent-up anger in the people we're manipulating.

Think of people you've frightened into doing what you want. Remember the panic in their eyes, the jittery nervousness while trying to please you, the mistakes they made under your pressure.

Or think of the tenseness you felt trying to maintain the image of perfection in the thing you were pressuring others to accomplish. Reflect on how strained the relationship became.

Most of all, grapple with what happened to your feelings about those people. The chances are, you lost your respect for them. It's difficult to admire people you can push around.

And yet, there are times when we can't help seeing that what people are doing is wrong, and we wish we could change them. Even if we give up our idea that we have either the right or the power to change people, we still long to help them. Especially if their actions and attitudes are making them ineffective, isolated, and unhappy.

The only way to help people change is to motivate them with love. That sounds great, but how do we do it? How do we become motivators? Where can we get guidance in helping other people reach their full potential as Christians?

The Christian Motivator's Guide: Romans 12:9–21

The best guide for motivating people I've ever found was written by the Apostle Paul. In Romans 12:9–21 Paul gives us the qualifications of an authentic Christian motivator. Those qualifications provide us with an incisive inventory of our own motivational skills. As we move through them, we will want to visualize the faces of the people we want to help. To what extent have we communicated these basic qualities?

1. Be Sure Love Is Your Incentive

The absolutely essential quality of an authentic motivator is love. "Let love be without hypocrisy," Paul says in verse nine. The kind of love he's talking about is the giving, forgiving, unqualified love he has received from Christ. We can't pretend to have that depth of love; it flows as a result of a profound relationship with the Lord.

In reality, *Christ is the master motivator.* It is from Him and how He has worked in our lives that we learn how to motivate and inspire others. He loved us when we least deserved it, and our resistance or rebellion did not dissuade His persistence in loving us.

Christ was more interested in our future than our past. He knew that the things we did were because of the kind of person we were inside. We couldn't change our actions until we were transformed. And our transformation didn't take place until we knew we were loved by Christ.

The important thing for us to remember is that *we* can't change anyone. Only Christ can do that. Instead, our function is to be so filled with Christ's love that we love with the power of His love. Notice that I didn't say copy His love. That's what Paul meant when he spoke of hypocritical love. A hypocrite is someone who is playing a part, pretending to be what he isn't. We are hypocritical lovers of people when we think that, on our own, we can imitate Christ's love. That's not our calling; we're simply riverbeds for the flow of His love.

Christ's love must transform our thinking about the person we want to motivate. He wants to help us see him or her as a forgiven, cherished person of ultimate value. Then He wants to help us envision that person's full potential, so we can claim the miracle of change He alone can perform. Once that's clearly implanted in our thinking, what we say to the person and how we relate to him or her will follow naturally.

Now comes the hard question. Do the people we'd like to motivate know how much we love them just as they are and that our love is not something we've manufactured but comes from Christ Himself?

"But," we object, "if we love people *as they are,* isn't there a danger that our acceptance will come across as approval of the very things they need to change?" Paul anticipated that question. In the same breath as he challenges us to love without hypocrisy, he says, "Abhor what is evil. Cling to what is good" (12:9).

We are called to unswerving moral purity in our own lives, but Paul emphasizes that at the same time we must care for those who fail. Like Christ, and with His power, we are to hate sin and love sinners. Effective motivators must do both. To help and influence other people, our attitudes and words must give them a vivid picture of what it means to live the abundant life in Christ to the fullest without feeling condemned.

Paul wrote that we are to cling to the good. The Greek word for "cling" means "join fast," "glue," "cement," "make one." A positive commitment to live the Ten Commandments plus a vigorous dedication to Christ-centered ethics is the best possible defense against evil. Our faith should be much more than a rules-oriented religion that is used as a basis for self-righteousness and judgment of others. Instead, it should be a magnetic example to others of the freedom and joy of a Christ-filled and empowered life.

To be attractive witnesses to the Good News of Jesus Christ, we must mirror God's grace. Without being guilty of unhealthy introspection, we must ask ourselves: "Am I living the quality of life I want to motivate in others? Does my love for them in spite of what they do or say make my witness dramatically irresistible?" It is true, of course, that people need to know where we stand. But they also need to know that we are committed to stand with them in their struggles.

Our love must be expressed in unfailing friendship. Being an understanding and caring friend may well be our most Christ-like act.

Friendship has become a lightweight word in our time. Not so in the Scriptures. It was the highest affirmation of Abraham that he was called a friend of God. Jesus ushered His disciples into a sublime level of intimacy when He said, "No longer do I call you servants, for a servant does not know what his master is doing; but I have called you friends" (John 15:15). And to be Christ's friend means befriending others.

Paul tells us the winsome way that this is to be communicated. "Be kindly affectionate to one another with brotherly love, in honor giving preference to one another; not lagging in diligence, fervent in spirit, serving the Lord" (Rom. 12:10–11). The last phrase puts befriending those we want to motivate on a dynamic level. Have you ever thought of service to the Lord in terms of being a friend to others?

Notice that Paul lists very specific ways to express that friendship. We are to be kind in communicating real affection for the people we want to help. That means telling people how important they are to us, how much we value them, and how fervently we believe in them and their potential.

We are to treat them as brothers or sisters who long for the Lord's best in their lives. Time with them is given high priority. Listening and caring about their needs honors them as persons.

We are to be available, quick to respond to their call for help without hesitation, "Not lagging in diligence" (Rom. 12:11). The word Paul uses for "lagging" means "slow" or "pokey." Night or day we are to be on call as truly reliable friends of those we are seeking to help and inspire.

Is this too much to ask? Not if we think of the people we're trying to help in the context of serving the Lord. That carries the impact of Jesus' words, "Inasmuch as you did it to one of the least of these My brethren, you did it to Me" (Matt. 25:40).

The thought that Christ may come to us in the very people who sometimes frustrate us the most—in the people we want to change—fills us with awe. How we respond to them is really our response to Christ. But the liberating assurance is that He will give us the love for people that's required to motivate them.

2. Pray for the People You Want to Motivate

The second great quality of an effective motivator is faithfulness in intercessory prayer. We need to spend more time talking to the Lord about a person we want to help than we spend talking to him or her! As Paul puts it in verse twelve, "Rejoicing in hope, patient in tribulation, continuing steadfastly in prayer."

Steadfast, consistent, prolonged prayer gives us both hope and patience. Praying for people helps us focus on what the Lord wants for them rather than on our ideas of what they should be or do. Intercessory prayer is not for the purpose of getting the Lord to accomplish our vision for people. Rather, we are to allow Him to show us what He wants to do in their lives.

So often my frustration over people has driven me to prayer for them. I usually begin by telling the Lord *my* agenda for them. Not surprisingly, that never works. But when I commit the people to Him and ask for His vision, what I begin to see is so much greater than my wishes. Then my prayers shift into high gear. I know that what I'm asking for is what the Lord is ready to give. I can rejoice in the hope that in His timing and way, it shall be so.

But not only does prayer clarify our hopes for people, it also gives us patience in the process of trying to help them. We need not be precipitate and resort to using fear tactics. At the same time we know that the Lord is at work in the people for whom we pray.

With infinite wisdom He's influencing people's thoughts, creating a desire to change. As He works His purpose out in circumstances, He is arranging opportunities and preparing the way for our efforts to encourage people. Christ will be with us to love through us, to inspire the right words, and to give us strength when we get discouraged. And our prayers for people will lead us to the next step of being a creative motivator.

3. Tangibilitate!

You'll not find the word "tangibilitate" in your dictionary. It was coined years ago by Father Divine in Harlem. One of his favorite, often-quoted sayings was, "The trouble in religion is that too many people know how to theorize and don't know how to 'tangibilitate.'"

It's not difficult to define the meaning of the word for our ministry of motivation. Do something tangible! We need to ask ourselves: What would communicate understanding and caring for the people we want to help? What can we do to lift some burden, meet some need, or provide some special delight? Paul talks about "distributing to the needs of saints, given to hospitality" (Rom. 12:13). He is asking his readers to meet physical needs and welcome people who are strangers. This is our model for all relationships.

Sometimes it means giving financial help or stepping in to assist in a crisis. More often it will be a sensitive, caring act that helps a person know you are committed to being a lasting friend. That can be everything from making a phone call to see how a person is doing, giving a meaningful gift, interrupting your schedule to listen, helping with a project, to including a person in the inner circle of your cherished friends at a special event.

A "tangibilitating" motivator is innovative. Rather than asking, "What can I do to help?" we take the time and effort to discover what would mean the most to the other person.

Recently, I spent one of the most delightful evenings of my life at a surprise party for a friend named John. A group of ten of us got together to express our gratitude to him. After the dinner in his honor, each of us had a chance to tell John how much we appreciated him for the countless ways he had expressed profound caring for us through the years. We represented a broad spectrum of backgrounds and professions. Though many of us did not know each other, we soon all became friends at the party because of our mutual appreciation for John.

The central theme of what we had to say to him was that he had motivated us to dare to be our best. Through the ups and downs of life John had always been an invaluable encourager. Some he had helped with personal crises, to others he had given hope in times of deep personal problems at home or work, and for others he had been a trusted confidant.

The high point of the evening was when John made his response. As part of it he repeated from memory the business and personal phone numbers of all of us. That's not a bit surprising. He calls often to spur us on or help lift the load of some need. Why are his calls always so timely? He prays a lot!

You may be thinking that John is probably a clergyman or a doctor. No, he's a very successful lawyer who, in addition to a busy practice that spans the nation, knows that his primary calling as a Christian is to motivate people with God's love.

4. Be an Affirmer

The fourth quality of a motivator is affirmation. It is the power to bless. Paul goes on in his list of attitudinal qualities of a Christian motivator with this challenge, "Bless those who persecute you; bless and do not curse" (Rom. 12:14). The word "bless" in Greek is *eulogeō*, meaning "speak well of" or "praise" (*eu* = well, *logos* = a word). If we are to speak well of those people on the fringes of our lives who make things difficult for us, we certainly should be careful to motivate those close to us with love and not manipulate them with fear.

What we say to or about a person has the power to bless or curse. And a lack of blessing is in itself a curse. It locks a person into his or her own present stage of growth. We all need affirmation of our worth as persons and our potential to be more than we are now. Affirmation provides self-esteem and hope for our future. It is not dishonest, fulsome flattery, but a communication that we are *for* people and not against them.

Words of affirmation from others are absolutely necessary to penetrate the layers of our own self-doubt and self-negation. We so easily get down on ourselves and become defensive. When others believe in us and encourage us by the blessing of affirmation, we are able to change and grow.

An affirmer is one who has experienced the ultimate affirmation of Christ. In spite of all that we've done and been, He loves us. He came to live and die for us that we might know that we are loved and forgiven. And now, as reigning Lord, God with us, He constantly reassures us that we belong to Him. He will never let us go.

When we know that, we can become affirmers of others even when they frustrate us. What they do cannot keep us from believing in what they can become by Christ's transforming power. Our trust is in what He will do; our only responsibility is to affirm that we love them.

A vital expression of our affirmation is to be involved with people in their times of delight and times of suffering. Paul encourages us to "rejoice with those who rejoice, and weep with those who weep" (12:15). Life is a bittersweet blend of success and failure, joy and sorrow. As genuine affirmers of other people, we are to be willing to share not only their mountain-peak experiences but their darkest valleys as well. Doing this leads us naturally to the next crucial aspect of motivation.

5. Focus the Vision

The central challenge of the Christian motivator is to help people envision what their lives would be like if committed to Christ, filled with His Spirit, and guided by His priorities and goals for them. Our task is not to bend them to our will or our ideas of what might be best for them. Instead, we are to ask penetrating questions that press them to evaluate where they are going in their lives, the kind of persons they want to be, and the quality of relationships they want to have. Our challenge is to help put people in touch with the Master.

Paul encourages us to "be of the same mind toward one another" (12:16). That really means "thinking the same thing," or "thinking together." This involves a blending of action and feelings. What we think about Christ and His will for us directly controls what we become. Therefore, truly creative motivators will inspire other people to allow Christ to repattern their minds in conformity with His will and purpose.

The secret of the transformation of human personality is receiving the mind of Christ. "Let this mind be in you which was also in Christ Jesus," Paul encouraged the Philippians (2:5). And to the Corinthian Christians he wrote, "For 'who has known the mind of the Lord that he may instruct Him?' But we have the mind of Christ" (1 Cor. 2:16). The mind of Christ is the motivating power for the reorientation of our thinking, the reformation of our wills, and the remolding of our feelings.

Too few Christians have discovered the gift of the in-dwelling mind of Christ. That's why our thinking about life is often so confused, our values and priorities are so incon-sistent with His, and our personalities are so far from being like Him. Any effort to motivate people to change or grow that skims over the deepest need we all have—to receive more of the mind of Christ—is surface meddling that brings no lasting results.

Often, problems and crises provide opportunities to talk with people about the direction and goals of their lives. The presence of conflict in our relationships should awaken us to be sensitive to the kinds of things we may be doing that would turn people off and stand in the way of their response to the Lord.

At times, however, there *is* a need for us to be graciously confrontive. The word "confront" has taken on some harsh baggage in our society. That's unfortunate because it really means "have face-to-face communication."

But any confrontation must always be preceded by caring and companionship. Only then can we share with people how Christ is working in our lives to deal with problems or challenges similar to theirs. It's then that they will feel free to ask themselves hard questions about their lives. And it's only when they have come to their own conclusions about their needs that we can lovingly share our hope and vision for them.

6. Be Vulnerable

In the dynamic process of motivating people, vulnerability about our own needs and discoveries is essential. Only a person who is changing can help others to change. No one has it all together. Anyone who tries to pretend that he has is disqualified as a motivator. In fact, we can reproduce in others only what we are constantly rediscovering in our own lives. And since the things that usually disturb us in others are the very things that either have been or are trouble spots in our own lives, we can readily recognize them and respond creatively.

Vulnerability makes us approachable. When we are free to share what the Lord is doing with the raw material of our imperfect personalities, people are drawn to us and feel free to share their lives with us. And since the Lord is never finished with us, there's always a next step of growth we need to take.

For example, in this chapter I've been trying to share some of the most liberating discoveries I've made about being a Christ-empowered motivator. With all my mind and heart, I believe that motivating people with love is the only alternative to manipulating them with fear.

And yet, living what I've written is one of the greatest challenges of my life. As a husband, father, manager of two large staffs for my church and media ministry, and as a concerned friend of many people I'd like to help, I'm constantly tempted to bypass the steps of motivation by love based on Paul's words in the twelfth chapter of Romans.

Sometimes, under the pressure of a busy schedule, I neglect my personal relationships with the very people I want to help. Then I wonder why my suggestions and advice are not well received. At such times, though, the Lord gently reminds me that my relationships with people I want to motivate must always be kept in good repair.

From this you can see that you and I are fellow strugglers in attempting to live without fear.

The other day, a friend who had worked with and for me as a fellow pastor introduced me to an audience as an impatient man with a vision. I was shocked. I like to think of myself as a patient person. Later my friend told me that what he had intended to communicate was that I express the urgency to press on in the renewal of the church and the preparation and training of Christians for ministry in the world.

The truth is I *am* an impatient person, in some less noble ways than my friend explained. I get impatient with the institutional process. I often want things done yesterday. And I tire of religious people who miss the adventure of exhilarating discipleship.

Usually, my impatience is caused by inner impatience with myself. That's when I must take an extra measure of time in my own prayers to receive fresh grace. The Lord is faithful: He reminds me of how patient He has had to be with me over the years. In these times of prayer I am refreshed and renewed to be a loving and vulnerable motivator of people.

Paul put it directly when he wrote, "Do not set your mind on high things, but associate with the humble. Do not be wise in your own opinion" (Rom. 12:16). The Apostle is not suggesting we give up our goals, but he is cautioning us about a false security in our own accomplishments. Instead, we are to "associate with the humble." The Greek actually means "be carried away with lowly things." In other words, we are to remember what the Lord has done for us and still needs to accomplish in us.

Believe me, the Lord has a way of knocking down our arrogant perfectionism by showing us what we really are. At such moments we become well aware that the kind of growth we are trying to inspire in others is also needed in our own lives. This leads us to the last quality of a motivator.

7. Never Give Up!

A Christ-inspired motivator never gives up. Knowing that the Master will never give up on us, we are not given the luxury of giving up on other people. Paul concludes his list of admonitions for the Christian communicator with three negative challenges that convey a very positive impact.

First, *don't retaliate.* "Repay no one evil for evil. Have regard for good things in the sight of all men. If it is possible, as much as depends on you, live peaceably with all men" (Rom. 12:17–18). For the Christian motivator this simply means that we are not to reject people who do not respond to our overtures of love. We can't write people off as long as the Lord has another chapter to write in their lives. We are to keep on praying, caring, and being available.

"To live peaceably" means to keep the relationship going, maintaining the channels of communication. Peace implies harmonious relationship. For me, that requires both timing and long-pull persistence. It's easy to win a battle by telling people how bad they are and lose the war of helping them claim how great they can be in Christ.

Second, *don't play God.* Paul says, "Beloved, do not avenge yourselves, but rather give place to wrath; for it is written, 'Vengeance is Mine, I will repay,' says the Lord" (12:19). This brings us full circle to where we began in our discussion of using fear to get what we want from people. When we threaten to punish or actually take judgment into our own hands, we not only lose our effectiveness to influence them positively, but we also provoke anger toward us that distracts people from coming to grips with what God wants to do in their lives.

I think that's what Paul has in mind when he quotes Proverbs 25:21–22. "Therefore, if your enemy hungers, feed him; if he thirsts, give him a drink; for in so doing you will heap coals of fire on his head" (12:20). Coals of fire symbolize the judgment, purification, and cleansing of God.

How does giving food and drink to our enemy do that? It simply dissipates their anger toward us and forces them to deal with God. Our persistence in personal and practical caring for people when they seem to deserve it the least can create a desire to know the Lord who is the source of our unconquerable love for them.

"Coals of fire" may also mean a burning conviction. Other Semitic proverbs refer to "coals in the heart" and "fire in the liver" as a flaming passion. It was a coal of fire from the altar that renewed Isaiah's vision and hope (Isa. 6:1–8). And in the New Testament fire is one of the central metaphors for the Holy Spirit. We are not far from that central meaning when we claim that our persistent love will be the spark that sets the fire of the Lord burning in another person.

Third, *don't give in to discouragement.* Paul says, "Do not be overcome by evil, but overcome evil with good" (12:21). Discouragement is Satan's most powerful weapon. His five most debilitating words are, "It won't make any difference."

Discouragement is really a build-up of fear. Far from being the problem of a few depressed people, discouragement lurks beneath the surface in most people. They need to know that we really believe the five most powerful words of a motivator, "Love makes all the difference!"

Each time we refuse to use fear to manipulate others, we overcome evil with good. Satan's program of trying to overcome good with fear is given one more defeat. Remember, we're counterculture Christians called to reverse the epidemic of fear in our world. The Lord is at work through us. Daily, He encourages us with signs of progress. We don't have to rely on fear.

So, don't underestimate the power of your ministry of motivation. Nothing is more important. It's why we were born and reborn. We don't have to be conduits of fear. We can be channels of love.

Step 12

I will give up the vague idea
that given time, things work out.
I will boldly face the future unafraid
with the sure confidence that God
will work all things together
for my ultimate good and His glory.

A Future
without Panic

"We did the best we could," the surgeon told John's family. "We got most of the malignancy, but as soon as John can take it, we're going to have to go back in after the rest of the malignancy."

I listened intently to the surgeon's report as I sat with John's family in a hospital waiting room after the first of several operations that saved his life.

The surgeon's words express my feelings as I begin this final chapter. We've been inside our minds and hearts, cutting away at the malignancy of fear that robs us of the joy of living. Now we must cut even more as we look ahead into the future.

Our fear of the future is not just caused by the uncertainty of what may happen tomorrow. It goes much deeper than that. A profound pessimism lurks inside most people. It's prompted by disappointment with a heresy that's shared by many Christians.

Simply stated, this heresy is expressed in a trite maxim.

"Given time, everything works out." I don't believe that. Nor do I believe that "time heals all wounds." This is little more than a sophisticated, but still blind, trust in fate. All too often we're guilty of saying to ourselves and others, "Don't worry, things have a way of working out." But sometimes things don't work out.

Many Christians who claim an assurance of heaven still have a deep fear about what's going to happen to them between now and the time of their physical death. Some feel victimized by seemingly uncontrollable events. We thank God for the good things that happen, but what about the pain and difficulties? When we've had what we would consider to be more than our share of problems, we fear that the future will simply be a further endurance contest.

A Key Verse: Romans 8:28

Kay felt that way. "I feel utterly defenseless," she said. "Up to this point I've felt that if I were patient, things would work out for the best. Now I'm at the end of my patience."

Do you ever feel that way? Do you look back over the deep troublesome valleys of your life and wonder, "Will the future hold anything more?" Then we take an extra large dose of the bromide that somehow things will work out. "Just hang in there," we urge ourselves. "Everything works out for those who wait. You've gotta believe the Bible—all things work together for good."

That sounds like good advice, doesn't it? Wrong! It's based on the wording of Romans 8:28 as it was translated in 1611 for our King James Version of the Bible. Many of us memorized that verse this way, "And we know that all things work together for good to them that love God, to them who are the called according to His purpose."

This wording places the emphasis on things working out in the lives of people who love God. That gave rise to this idea that given enough time, things will work out. And the next step was the development of the vague trust in eventuality rather than in God.

This panic-inducing idea about the future, however, loses that meaning when we understand that in the original Greek the order of the words in this verse puts the meaning in true perspective and gives us a cure for our fear of the future. "For we know that to those who love God, in all things God works together for good to those who are called according to His purpose."

Things don't work out; God works out things! That truth not only contradicts the current heresy but fills us with courage and expectancy for the rest of our lives on earth. It also paves the way to our twelfth and final step in living without fear: *I will give up the vague idea that given time, things work out. I will boldly face the future unafraid with the sure confidence that God will work all things together for my ultimate good and His glory.*

God Is Our Future

Let's begin where Paul did in his words of assurance for the Christians in Rome. God is our future. He created us to receive and return His love. In Christ, He reconciled us to Himself so that we could know and love Him. We couldn't do that on our own.

Saint Augustine had this truth in mind when he prayed, "Give what Thou asketh and ask what Thou wilt." When Christ takes up residence in our minds and hearts, He loves the Father through us. He gives us the freedom to claim His gift of our family likeness with Him.

We have been chosen by God and called to live with trusting confidence in His goodness. The future is a gift in which Christ accomplishes His purpose in and through us. And what is God's purpose? It is to make us like His Son!

When we commit ourselves to becoming like Christ, we begin the process of liberation from our fear of the future. Everything else must be secondary. No person, plan, or program can be placed ahead of this goal. When this becomes our sole purpose in life, we become the special focus of the Father's fear-dispelling love. By grace alone, we are able to participate in the love between the Father and the Son. Christ in us gives us the power to truly love the Father. That love qualifies us to be counted among the people Paul calls "those who love God."

How God Works

Just as God arranged circumstances to bring us to the place of willingness to receive Christ, so, too, He uses all of life to help us grow in Christ. He entrusts the management of that to His Son.

Christ is with us watching over all that happens to us. He goes before us to guide us each step into the future. He is beside us as our Companion and Friend, and He is behind us to gently prod us when we lag behind with caution and reluctance. Most of all, Christ is in our minds to help us understand the purpose of what happens to and around us. Moment by moment, He shows us that He is using the events of life to strengthen in us the fiber of His nature and character.

I don't think we have to wait until the end of our lives to understand why we have experienced life's dark threads as well as the threads of gold and silver. If we come to the Lord with an open, receptive mind, He will give us exactly the insight we need to understand His deeper purpose in our circumstances. He interprets what happened the day before and inspires us to trust Him for the day ahead. And for anything He chooses not to interpret now, He gives us the quiet assurance to wait. I like the way William Cowper expressed this assurance:

God's purposes will ripen fast
Unfolding every hour
The bud may have a bitter taste
But sweet will be the flower.
God is His own Interpreter
And He will make it plain.

God Uses Everything

The crucial truth the Lord, our Interpreter, wants to make plain is that He will use everything that happens to us for the accomplishment of His awesome purpose. That's what He impressed on Paul's mind and validated in the Apostle's experience.

At the end of his third missionary journey, around A.D. 57, Paul could look back and see how the Lord had been orchestrating the events of his life. Nothing had been wasted. The triumphs and the tragedies had been used to mold the clay of his nature into the image of Christ. Paul had known success and failure, victory and defeat, acclaim and rejection.

Only one thing can account for Paul's resiliency and his confidence for the future. The years had taught him well that, "All things God works together for good to those who are the called according to His purpose."

We can't face the future without fear until we are absolutely sure of that truth. Of course, we still make mistakes, bring problems on ourselves, and resist the Lord's best for our lives. But there is just no way one can face the future with confidence without the firm hope that the Lord will make the best of our efforts and help us to grow through our failures.

At the same time it is important we understand that not all of our problems are of our own making. Often we are victims of other people's ineptness or confused motives. Our future is peopled with the full spectrum of proud, selfish, competitive, greedy humankind. Our tomorrows will be invaded by conflict and broken relationships. But we can endure the people problems if only we know for sure that the Lord will help us and that he will use even the difficulties to deepen our relationship with Him.

And our assurance that He will use all things for our growth and His glory must also extend to the realities of pain, sickness, and death. In it all, we will need to know that He is both our healer and our strength to endure. We will know His miraculous interventions and His patience when we need to wait. Mysteriously, He will use our times of physical weakness to teach us to depend on Him. And when we walk through the valley of the shadow of death, He will be there to lead us all the way to heaven.

Neither the crafty influences of evil nor the calamities of the natural world will be beyond the Lord's power to utilize for our good. He will be with us to help us overcome evil and to trust Him in the tragedies. Nothing can separate us from Him or His creative purposes for us.

Works Together

You see, believing that God works all things together for good does not exempt us from the difficulties of life, but it does assure us of exceptional power in handling them. It helps to remember that God does not send trouble to force us to grow. There's already an abundance of trouble in this fallen, rebellious world that refuses to accept His sovereignty. And yet, in spite of humankind's rejection of Him, He rules and overrules to protect, guide, and care for "those who are the called according to His purpose."

The way the Lord "works things together for good" is to block us from getting into some troubles, strengthen us in others, and turn still others into stepping stones. Nothing escapes His loving providence. He is constantly working to increase our joys and strengthen us in our difficulties.

The Greek verb for "works together" also means "to work

with." The Lord not only works things together with perfect timing for our good, but He works with us in helping us understand what He is doing in and through us. We discover that often it is in life's tight places, troublesome problems, and painful experiences that we have made the longest strides in our growth as people.

That's the confidence that cures our fears of the future. We are promised neither a trouble-free future nor one in which *things* will eventually work out. What we are promised is that God will work all things together with creative continuity for our ultimate good. Tomorrow is under His control. We don't have to try to hold back the dawn or flinch at the problems it may bring.

We can rest comfortably with the assurance that God knows what He's doing! He's with us in Christ. And the Master whispers in our hearts, "Don't be anxious about tomorrow. God will take care of your tomorrow, too. Live one day at a time" (Matt. 6:34, TLB).

New Every Morning

The conviction that God uses everything and brings His best for us out of the worst that might happen must be reaffirmed every morning. Some great verses to repeat the moment we wake up are found in Lamentations 3:22–24. Start your day with this mind-opener about God: "His compassions fail not. They are new every morning; great is Your faithfulness. 'The Lord is my portion' says my soul, 'Therefore I hope in Him!'"

I've repeated that daily for years. Beginning the morning that way has helped me to remember that the Lord has enabled me to grow through problems and make my most exciting discoveries while wrestling with the difficulties. That's especially helpful when I wake up tense, with a problem I have to face that day weighing heavily on my mind.

One morning a few months ago I awoke with a big problem on my mind. My stomach was knotted with feelings of fear. Fear gripped my emotions. Then I repeated Jeremiah's affirmation of God's faithfulness. After that, I lay in bed going over what might happen. However bad it might be, I knew from experience that the Lord would use it. So I began to praise Him for what I was going to learn through the problem. Only then did the fear subside. I felt new strength to get up and tackle the problem.

All through the day, as I faced the problem head-on, I kept praying, "Lord, what are You trying to teach me in this? What good do You want to bring out of it?" As it turned out, the Lord not only helped me find a solution to the problem but used what I had been through to help someone else.

That evening, I had dinner with David, a good friend and member of my church. "Lloyd," he said, "what do you do when you are awakened at four in the morning feeling fearful over what's ahead in the day? I feel like I want to cancel the day, turn off the alarm clock set for six o'clock, pull the covers over my head, and just not get up."

David confided that lately he'd had a lot of mornings like that. He told me between four and six had become what he called "worry time." Problems were magnified as he dramatized in his mind all the terrible things that might happen.

I shared with David what I'd been through that very day and the fresh experience I'd had of seeing the Lord bring good out of a worrisome problem.

"David," I said, "it sounds like we are soul brothers. Why don't we covenant to pray for each other that we will turn our early morning worry time into praise time? When a problem wakes us up, let's give it to the Lord and spend our time praying about the best He could bring out of it rather than the worst we can imagine. Then let's claim the vision He gives us and thank Him that He will work it all out in His timing and way."

David and I get together from time to time to check in

with each other. The last time we were together he said, "Do you know what? I think the Lord has pulled off an old-fashioned miracle in this crusty ol' Presbyterian. The other day I realized that my feelings of dread about the future are completely gone!"

The secret of David's liberation came in recognizing that all his fears were related to secondary things—his family, health, job, and reputation. He needed to focus on God's goal for his life. And when he did that, he became confident that God would work all the secondary concerns together to accomplish that goal.

God's Grand Plan for Our Lives

The only sure way to overcome our fear of the future is to make God's "good" our goal. God doesn't work all things together just to set us free from fear. That's a by-product of committing our lives to His plan and submitting to His agenda for fulfilling it.

We've come full circle from where we began: the good for which God works everything together is to make us like Christ. We don't need to fear anything that might happen to us in the future, because we belong to God. He will not allow anything to happen that He will not use for His plan. God never gives up on us or on His purpose in us.

That was Paul's conviction as he neared the end of his life in prison in Rome. We suspect the message he communicated to the Christians in Rome was what he also wrote to the Philippian Christians. The believers in both churches were afraid. They faced opposition, persecution, and discouragement. In response, Paul shared the steadfast confidence he had for himself and for them. "Being confident of this very thing," he wrote to the Philippian Christians, "that He who has begun a good work in you will complete it until the day of Jesus Christ" (1:6).

The "good work" the Lord had begun in Paul and the

early Christians was the same as the "good" for which He was working all things together: the miracle of shaping them into the image of Christ. That's His plan and purpose. What the Lord has begun in us, He will complete. All the resources of heaven and the present ministry of Christ Himself are committed to assure us of victory. Once His "good work" has begun in us, He will use all the outer trials we face to build up our inner person. He provides exactly what we need each day.

Billy Graham discovered this early in his ministry. Just before he began his crusades many years ago in Los Angeles, he attended a conference sponsored by the First Presbyterian Church of Hollywood at Forest Home in the San Bernardino Mountains. Dr. Henrietta Mears, the Director of Christian Education of our church at that time, had a strong influence on his life. Dr. Graham has written about what that time at Forest Home meant to him as he experienced the Lord's power to press on in the full realization of the "good work" that the Lord had begun in him.

"My faith was a wavering variety, and I came to the place where I was in no position to help others while I myself was so faltering. This greatly disturbed me.

"One day, at a retreat for young people, I went out into the woods to meditate and pray. I made up my mind that on that day I would either give up what little Christian faith I had or discover a stronger base upon which to stand for Christ. I opened the Bible and this verse caught my attention: 'He who has begun a good work in you will complete it till the day of Jesus Christ.' It dawned upon me that what faith I had was a gift of God, that His reserves were boundless, that if I would consent to receive, He was ready, willing, and able to keep on giving. From that day to this, He has never stopped giving and performing that which He has begun."

Since that time, Dr. Graham has preached to millions of people, and hundreds of thousands have been converted to

Christ through his love-motivated preaching. The "good work" the Lord began has never stopped growing in greater power and effectiveness.

The Focus of Our Attention

Fear of the future invades our minds and hearts when we focus on the evil around us and not on Christ and what He is doing to complete God's "good work" in us. Actually the fear we feel is like a bell on a channel buoy. It rings to alert us that we are off course.

I've never known it to fail. When I worry about the future, that's the time the Lord breaks through. By helping me to trust Him more, He leads me to a bold new step in experiencing the "character transplant" of Christ's life in me.

Then the truths I've held in a vague way become my experience, and I can pray for myself the prayer Paul prayed for the Philippian Christians. "And this I pray, that your love may abound still more and more in knowledge and all discernment, that you may approve the things that are excellent, that you may be sincere and without offense . . . being filled with the fruits of righteousness which are by Jesus Christ, to the glory and praise of God" (1:9–11).

Note the progression in the prayer. The Lord's overflowing love makes us able to understand and experience His faithfulness and goodness in all that happens to us. The word for "knowledge" that Paul uses is "experienced truth" as opposed to "conceptual ideas." We can be aware of the Lord's presence in spite of the difficulties we encounter.

That motivates us to seek His excellence, the highest potential for our growth in all things. Then, we long to cooperate in the continued development of His "good work" in us, and we are sincere about pressing on.

The Greek word for "sincere" means "judged by the sunlight," while its Latin counterpart means "without wax," and is used for a piece of pottery in which the imperfections had not been filled with wax to make the piece look perfect. For us, sincerity is holding our lives up to the light of Christ, being thankful for our growth so far and not trying to cover up our needs. We can be honest and open about our next steps of growth in becoming like Christ. Happily, He is not finished with us: we are not what we were, and thanks to Him, what we are is only the beginning of what He has planned for us.

Contagious Faith

Paul vividly illustrates from his own life how the Lord can use everything to help us grow and then use us to encourage others who fear the future. "I want you to know, brethren, that the things which happened to me have actually turned out for the furtherance of the gospel" (Phil. 1:12). He goes on to explain that his imprisonment had given him opportunities to lead the guards to Christ and had given new boldness to the Christians in Rome.

While Paul was imprisoned, the guards were chained to him. Imagine being chained to the Apostle Paul! It has been said that the guards had to be relieved of that duty because they were becoming Christians as a result of prolonged contact with Paul while chained to him. The guards came to realize that, in reality, Paul was bonded to Christ. And that liberating bondage made Paul the most free person in history. His faith was contagious. Even in difficult circumstances, the "good work" of the Lord in Paul continued to grow.

Assurance

The same is true for us. Our confidence is not that things work out, but that God works out things!

And with that assurance we can retake our twelve steps to living without fear. I've never outgrown my need to review them daily and claim the Lord's power for each bold step. As I do, the Lord reminds me of His fear-conquering presence.

Fear not, I am with you. I will never leave or forsake you. You are Mine for eternity.

Seek to please only Me, and you'll have nothing and no one to fear.

Face your fears, retrace them to their root in your soul, displace them with My indwelling presence, and erase them with an assurance of My forgiving love.

Love yourself as I love you. I have healed your frightening memories. My love casts out fear.

You don't have to worry about being inadequate ever again. I am your strength, wisdom, and courage.

When others reject you, be sure of My unqualified love for you.

Let go of your own control and humbly trust Me to guide you each step of the way.

You have the gift of imagination to picture and live My best for your life.

Don't spend your life worrying about sickness and death—live your life to the fullest now.

You don't need fear to manipulate people any more. You are free to motivate them with love.

And be sure of this—the "good work" I have begun in you will be completed. You have nothing to fear. I love you!

Notes

Chapter 1
[1]The account of this recurring dream was told to *Time* magazine writer Richard Corlis and appeared as part of an article on Oliver Stone in the January 16, 1987 issue of *Time* magazine.

Chapter 2
[1]*Los Angeles Times,* 21 November 1986, part V, p. 20.

Chapter 5
[1]R. C. Sproul, quoted in "Harry and the Humble Habit" by Steve Brown, *Christian Life,* October 1986, p. 30.

Chapter 7
[1]For additional information about the life of Amy Carmichael, see *Amy Carmichael of Dohnavar* by Frank Houghton (Ft. Washington, PA: Christian Literature Crusade, 1979).
[2]Elisha A. Hoffman, "I Must Tell Jesus." Copyright 1893, renewed 1926.
[3]"Tell Me Again Lord, I Forget" by Ruth Harms Calkin. Tyndale House Publishers, Inc., © 1986. Used by permission.

Chapter 8
[1]Adelaide Pollard, "Have Thine Own Way, Lord," 1902.

Chapter 9
[1]James Weldon Johnson, "Listen Lord—A Prayer," in *God's Trombones* (New York: Viking Press, Inc., 1927). Used by permission.
[2]Words and music by Paul Baskin. Copyright 1987. Used by permission.

Chapter 10
[1]I highly recommend Amy Harwell's outstanding book, *When Your Friend Gets Cancer: How You Can Help* (Wheaton, IL: Harold Shaw Pub., 1987). She explains what she discovered and how to help others who face cancer.